OLD TESTAMENT GUIDE

General Ed

R.N

AMOS

College London (KQC) Library

AMOS

A. G. Auld

Published by JSOT Press
for the Society for Old Testament Study

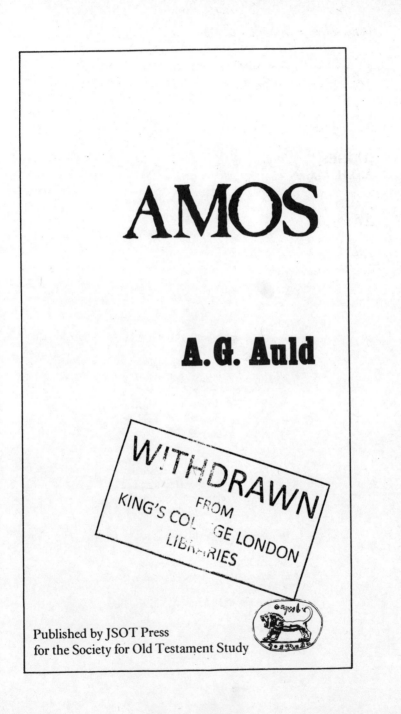

For my Dartmouth students:
Betsy, Harry, Marge
Mary and Mary Jane

Copyright © 1986 JSOT Press

Published by
JSOT Press
Department of Biblical Studies
The University of Sheffield
Sheffield S10 2TN
England

Typeset by JSOT Press
Printed in Great Britain
by Dotesios (Printers) Ltd
Bradford-on-Avon, Wiltshire

British Library Cataloguing in Publication Data

Auld, A. Graeme
Amos.—(Old Testament guides, ISSN
0264-6498)
1. Bible. O.T. Amos—Commentaries
I. Title   II. Series
224′.806   BS1585.3

ISBN 1-85075-005-X

CONTENTS

PREFACE

I have appreciated the invitation of the editors of JSOT Press to contribute to their series of Old Testament Guides. My thinking on the book of Amos has developed over several years under the stimulus of classes in New College, Edinburgh. However, the first draft of the present volume was prepared in the summer months of 1984 in the delightful setting of Dartmouth College, New Hampshire, as I discussed the interpretation of Amos with a small and able seminar group. To them the volume is dedicated.

Particular thanks are due to the Editor of these Old Testament Guides. Professor Whybray has made suggestions and taken pains beyond the normal bounds of duty. With his care, the volume has been very much improved.

ABBREVIATIONS

AOAT	Alter Orient und Altes Testament, Neukirchen-Vluyn: Neukirchener Verlag
BZ	*Biblische Zeitschrift*
BZAW	Beihefte zur ZAW
CBQ	*Catholic Biblical Quarterly*
CUP	Cambridge University Press
EvTh	*Evangelische Theologie*
FRLANT	Forschungen zur Religion und Literatur des Alten und Neuen Testaments, Göttingen: Vandenhoeck & Ruprecht
FS	Festschrift
HTR	*Harvard Theological Review*
HUCA	*Hebrew Union College Annual*
ICC	International Critical Commentary, Edinburgh: T. & T. Clark
JB	Jerusalem Bible
JBL	*Journal of Biblical Literature*
JNES	*Journal of Near Eastern Studies*
JSOT	*Journal for the Study of the Old Testament*
JSOTS	JSOT Supplement
KAT	Kommentar zum Alten Testament, Gütersloh: Gerd Mohn
LXX	Septuagint
MT	Masoretic Text
NEB	New English Bible
OTS	*Oudtestamentische Studiën*
RSV	Revised Standard Version
SOTS	Society for Old Testament Study
SVT	Supplements to *Vetus Testamentum*
VT	*Vetus Testamentum*
WMANT	Wissenschaftliche Monographien zum Alten und Neuen Testament, Neukirchen-Vluyn: Neukirchener Verlag
ZAW	*Zeitschrift für die alttestamentliche Wissenschaft*
ZDPV	*Zeitschrift des Deutschen Palästina-Vereins*

INTRODUCTION

AMOS IS a book to which many people turn early in any serious engagement with Old Testament studies. And it is easy in fact to understand its contemporary popularity. Its tones of social protest, religious critique, and universalism are immediately perceived, and enjoy perennial appeal—at least in the modern world. It is an important source for the claim that ancient Israel's classical prophets had a fundamental concern with social justice; and accordingly it reinforces the 'manifesto' of liberation theology.

Its contents are varied, yet handled within manageable length. And, for those who are learning Hebrew, its relatively straightforward text and recurring formulaic presentation leave some small place in the memory for attention to a few critical matters!

Critical issues are in reasonable supply. This volume ought to be clear enough witness to that fact! Yet they do not obtrude: they are varied and well-spaced through the text, and the general sense of a passage is seldom in fundamental doubt. That too makes Amos a good book for introductory study.

1. The opening two chapters lead the reader to Israel slowly through a full tour of seven neighbours. Their rhetoric is impressive both in its near-regularity and in its effective variety. Amos's assault on Israel when it comes seems all the more biting because of its delay, and because of our surprise that Israel should have been put on a level with the peoples round about.

The detailed and almost inexorable critiques of group after group in the central chapters 3–6 are withering in their tersely economical presentation. Again and again Amos takes up an ironical lament over sections of the population as if they were already dead, or as good as finished. The general tone of these chapters is barely relieved by the single 'perhaps' in 5.15—'perhaps the Lord God of Hosts may be gracious to the *remnant* of Joseph'. And even that relief has a bitter sting in its tail, as we shall see in Chapter 7 below.

The visions that open each of the final three chapters engage our imagination, and offer an important clue to Amos's self-consciousness in his role and possibly to the means by which he came to his convictions. The picture painted in the midst of these visions (7.10-17) of a farmer resolutely standing his ground before the (High) Priest of Bethel, who is of course a royal appointee, has wide appeal however dangerous a precedent it may seem to senior officials.

And the closing verses (9.11-15) send their readers away with hearts a little less heavy: clutching again at hope rather than despair, and grateful that mercy is the last word to Israel and to the Davidic house rather than near-unmitigated warning.

Israel in the context of the nations, the lack of justice and righteousness in Israel and the threat of punishing invasion, visions of the divine resolve and the consequences for a human spokesman, and hope for a fresh start in the future: these are the recurring stuff of the prophetic books of the Old Testament. But seldom within these books are the themes just listed so discretely handled or so readily separable. This too makes Amos a good point of departure for a survey of that whole section of the biblical canon.

2. It may be useful at this point to explain the plan of my own approach to Amos in this volume. It is not just out of perversity (I hope) that I have chosen not to allow the elements of my introduction to mirror the progression of the themes in the book itself. I have started near the end, with reports of Amos's visions and the discussion of his status, rather than at the beginning because I find that much reading of the Bible's prophetic literature is prejudiced since readers *know* in advance what a prophet or visionary *really* is—but are wrong. The best way to combat this is not to talk in generalities; that is part of the problem. It is to make a detailed scrutiny of those very passages in Amos which report visions or talk about prophesying.

If we move next to Israel in the context of her neighbouring nations, it is not just because this is where Amos begins, or because oracles against the nations are a frequent element in prophetic books. The opening two chapters of the book contain crucial evidence of the rhetorical style of Amos and concerning the unity of the book of Amos. Fortified by these chapters of close textual argument, we turn to more general discussion of 'literary' issues in the book as a whole.

The more familiar topic of social and religious critique comes next, with a review of the relevant texts, and a discussion of some of the wider issues they raise. Then the concluding chapter discusses aspects of the religious and theological significance of the book.

3. Student and teacher alike are generously served by the profusion of published studies available. Fuller details of the main resources are given at the end of this chapter. The serious middle-length commentaries in English by Hammershaimb and Mays remain very fresh a decade and a half after publication, and attractively different. The opening chapter of the rather earlier volume by Watts remains a very good orientation to study of Amos. The more weighty German commentaries of Wolff and Rudolph have raised to a new intensity scholarly discussion of the options of slow growth (on the one side) or substantial unity (on the other) of this book. (Wolff's work, perhaps the more adventurous of the two, is also available in English dress.)

More recent—and very readable—contributions have advanced this discussion on both sides. Coote has followed Wolff's lead with a forceful re-presentation of the case for three main stages (and periods) in the formation of the book. Then the relevant section of Koch's account of the Prophets of the Assyrian Period urges a much more unitary approach to the text than has been common in German critical circles. This chapter by Koch on Amos is only a summary of a much larger case. For Professor Koch led a team of researchers in Hamburg who subjected this short prophetic text to near microscopic examination, and published *in three volumes* their examination of Amos 'by the methods of a structural form-criticism'.

As if that sort of research is not daunting enough, the annotated bibliography of studies on Amos between 1800 and 1983 recently published by van der Wal runs to 177 pages, and comprises some 1,100 articles or books! However my purpose in mentioning this is not at all to scare beginners, but rather to assure them that they are embarking on a study that many before them have found both vital and fascinating. Van der Wal's work simply shows at a glance that the studies I mentioned earlier are merely the most readily available and noticeable tip of a much larger and untidily shaped iceberg of publications. They offer a useful means of access and preliminary orientation. And of course my own natural bias as yet another author helps me to claim that the bewildering plethora of relevant publications makes this new introduction *more* rather than *less* necessary!

Two article-length contributions of more recent years seem to me to deserve particular commendation, if only because many beginners will not have ready access to them. The one is Peter Ackroyd's discussion of the links between Amos's short altercation with Amaziah (Amos 7.10-17) and two other biblical narratives: the story of the man of God from Judah in 1 Kings 13 on the one side, and the brief account of another royal 'counsellor' in 2 Chronicles 25 on the other. (This was published in an American volume now out of print.) The second is Hartmut Gese's magisterial account of 'Composition in Amos' (published in German).

The most important publication to come to hand during preparation of this volume is Hans Barstad's substantial monograph on *The Religious Polemics of Amos*. He seeks to counter the prevailing opinion that ethics is the basic content of the prophet's message, and argues that Amos is a foremost exponent of an ideological and cultural struggle between 'Yahwism' and 'Baalism'.

4. Amos is an exciting book to study: and not just for its own sake. Amos is widely held to be the earliest of the so-called 'writing prophets'. Inasmuch as he is a *first*, we are freed from attention to his immediate predecessors. Yet precisely because he is the first of an apparently novel group of eighth-century thinkers (Amos, Hosea, Isaiah, Micah), whatever we can deduce about him will inevitably influence our study of the others.

But there is a much more fascinating and important dimension to contemporary study of the book of Amos. In today's very fluid state of Old Testament scholarship, many old certainties have been dissolved. Many writers are far less confident that sizeable strands of the Pentateuch and Joshua–Samuel took shape as early as the tenth and ninth centuries BCE. And in such a situation a securely dated and historical Amos would be an indispensable benchmark and point of reference. That adds to the urgency of our discussion of the unity and development of the book associated with his name. Just how much of the text is in fact serviceable for a reconstruction of the thought and activity of the *historical* Amos of the middle of the eighth century BCE?

5. Our last 'introductory' words should be about Amos's historical setting. It is widely held first of all that his role on Israel's stage was a brief one. The book's own title talks of activity 'two years before the earthquake'. Few scholars have detected evidence of development and rethinking in the words of Amos; and so his public utterances

could well have been delivered in such a two-year period or less. One scholar has even reorganized the material of the book into a single long sustained address. Unfortunately we know nothing now of that earthquake which was once memorable enough to date other events by.

The Israel Amos addressed was the northern of the two sister kingdoms of Judah and Israel which co-existed sometimes more and sometimes less amicably in the two centuries after King Solomon's death (922–722 BCE). Amos 1.1 locates the 'earthquake' in the period when Uzziah was king of Judah and Jeroboam king of Israel. Unhappily this information too is much less specific than we would like; for each king ruled for some 40 years, and their long reigns largely overlapped.

It is often supposed that Amos's short prophetic career was in the later part of the period defined by these kings' reigns (roughly 780–740 BCE)—that is, around the middle of the century. The discussion starts by noting that Israel had enjoyed a considerable measure of peace and stability under Jeroboam's long stewardship; and goes on to argue that such tranquillity had made possible the upper-class luxury which Amos castigated so effectively. This may be the case. However, the Dutch scholar de Geus has recently reevaluated biblical poverty in the light of archaeological excavation of material remains in Israel and Palestine. We shall see in a later chapter that this evidence suggests to him that a general economic decline had already begun to affect Israel and Judah in the earlier ninth century BCE. If this is so, then the conventional lever for exerting some purchase on the date of Amos's proclamation may have proved too slender. The disparity between rich and poor which Amos found so objectionable may have been the result, not of recent prosperity acquired by some under Jeroboam's long reign, but of a longer established decline which bore most heavily on the poor.

Locating Amos in his proper time and plotting his career against historical coordinates is a vital task. Two factors both complicate it and make the attempt more necessary. The one is that many elements in Amos resonate with other biblical passages: Gilgal, with the stories of Joshua and Saul, and also with the words of Amos's contemporary Hosea; Bethel, with so many other memories of that sanctuary, but especially its choice by the earlier Jeroboam as one of his royal state temples; Jeroboam himself, with his earlier namesake, the arch-bogeyman of the books of Kings who had broken away from the house of David and temple of Solomon.

The other is that so many of Amos's words are immediately relevant to so many situations he never envisaged, that the precise circumstances of their first delivery seem almost irrelevant. Indeed we may suppose that they have been remembered and preserved partly because they were more generally applicable.

Further Reading

The standard contemporary commentaries in English are:

E. Hammershaimb, *The Book of Amos*, Oxford: Blackwell, 1970.

J.L. Mays, *Amos* (Old Testament Library), London: SCM Press, 1969.

H.W. Wolff, *Joel and Amos* (Hermeneia), Philadelphia: Fortress Press, 1977. (This is a translation of the German BK, XIV/2.)

The standard English work of an earlier generation was:

W.R. Harper, *Amos and Hosea* (ICC), 1905.

With Wolff, the other large-scale contemporary German work is:

W. Rudolph, *Joel, Amos, Obadja, Jona* (KAT XIII/2), 1971.

Two recent and very serviceable introductions to the prophetic literature are:

J. Blenkinsopp, *A History of Prophecy in Israel*, London: SPCK, 1984.

K. Koch, *The Prophets*, 2 vols. London: SCM Press, 1982/3.

Koch's fresh account of Amos in the book just listed represents a popular presentation of the results achieved in his *Amos. Untersucht mit den Methoden einer strukturalen Formgeschichte* (AOAT 30), 1976.

The two major treatments in English which both undermine the old Greek adage that 'a big book is a big pain' are:

J. Lindblom, *Prophecy in Ancient Israel*, Oxford: Blackwell, 1962.

G. von Rad, *Old Testament Theology* II, Edinburgh: Oliver & Boyd, 1965.

Orientation on Amos is expertly provided in:

J.D.W. Watts, *Vision and Prophecy in Amos*, Leiden: E.J. Brill, 1958.

H.W. Wolff, *Amos the Prophet*, Philadelphia: Fortress Press, 1973.

A.S. van der Woude, 'Three Classical Prophets: Amos, Hosea and
Micah', in R. Coggins, A. Phillips & M. Knibb (eds.)
Israel's Prophetic Tradition, CUP, 1982, 32-57.

This last-mentioned volume of 'Essays in Honour of Peter Ackroyd' entitled
Israel's Prophetic Tradition is an exemplary collection of complementary and
up-to-date studies. The contributions of Whybray, Phillips, and Sawyer also
have relevance to the study of Amos.

The other recent important discussions of Amos in English referred to in this
chapter are:

P.R. Ackroyd, 'A Judgment Narrative between Kings and Chronicles?
An Approach to Amos 7.9-17', G.W. Coats & B.O. Long
(eds.), *Canon and Authority*, Philadelphia: Fortress Press,
1977, 71-87.
H.M. Barstad, *The Religious Polemics of Amos* (SVT 34), 1984.
R.B. Coote, *Amos among the Prophets: Composition and Theology*,
Philadelphia: Fortress Press, 1981.
H. Gese, 'Komposition bei Amos', *Congress Volume, Vienna 1980*
(SVT 32), 1981, 74-95.

Many of the studies already listed have useful bibliographies; however, in
completeness these are quite overshadowed by:

A. van der Wal, *Amos: A Classified Bibliography*, Amsterdam: VU
boekhandel/uitgeverij, 1983.

Connections between Amos and Isaiah are explored in:

R. Fey, *Amos und Jesaja* (WMANT 12), 1963, 144-47.

The attempt to reconstruct a single speech from the given text of Amos i

J. Morgenstern, 'Amos Studies IV', *HUCA* 32 (1961), 300-13.

General historical background can be found in any of the standard
handbooks on the history of Israel, such as those by Bright, Herrmann,
Noth, and Soggin. Useful archaeological comments are made in:

J.K. de Geus, 'Die Gesellschaftskritik der Propheten und die
Archäologie', *ZDPV* 98 (1982), 50-57.

Some of the articles and monographs in German which have achieved
almost classical status in recent discussion of Amos are:

H. Graf Reventlow, *Das Amt des Propheten bei Amos* (FRLANT
80), 1962.
R. Smend, 'Das Nein des Amos', *EvTh* 23 (1963), 404-23.
E. Würthwein, 'Amos-Studien', *ZAW* 62 (1950), 10-52.

1

AMOS
THE VISIONARY

IT IS AS a visionary that the Book of Amos presents its hero. The title verse talks of the words *which* Amos *saw*, or alternatively of an Amos *who saw*. (Hebrew does not possess specific relative pronouns, but an all-purpose relative 'marker' which occasionally leaves matters ambiguous.) And *seer* is what in 7.12 Amaziah calls Amos, the troublemaker within his temple precincts. But more important than a summary introduction or an epithet flung by an official, the final third of the book has at its very core a series of five visions presented in a first-person report.

In their very language for 'seeing', these visions are different from the other two expressions just noted. The key-word of these reports is *ra'ah*. This is the common word in Hebrew for 'seeing' and 'looking', although it also can express heightened perception and 'second sight'. On the other hand 'saw' in the title and 'seer' in Amaziah's words use *ḥazah*, which is almost never found outside stereotyped official usage.

1. The Structure of Amos's Visions

It is unnecessary here to rehearse the reasons for the unanimous view that it is two *pairs* of vision-reports (7.1-3/4-6 and 7.7-9/8.1-3) that precede the fifth and last. However a number of related questions are contentious: (a) do 7.9 and 8.3 have an integral relationship with 7.7-8 and 8.1-2, or are they later supplements? (b) is the fifth vision (9.1-4) the original conclusion to the series, or a later addition?

a. In the first two visions (7.1-3, 4-6) Amos is 'shown' or 'let *see*' two nightmarish images. In the earlier of these a plague of locusts is consuming the crop, and it is the more terrible, because this is already the second and final crop of the season. The first is already in the royal barns: this later harvest was required for local consumption. Amos in his vision cannot remain a mute spectator, and asks forgiveness for Jacob, who is 'so small'. This secures a divine change of mind.

In the second, there is a move from what we would call 'natural' disaster to a calamity of cosmic proportions. The divine fire has licked dry the great deeps below the earth, and proceeds to destroy the land itself, when the dreamer interrupts his dream with a cry for God to stop because of Jacob's smallness, and is assured that this too shall not be. In several formal respects these two visions are a *pair*; but the two images presented do not amount to the *same* thing. There is movement and development from the first to the second. 'Forgive' (v. 2) becomes the more desperate 'stop' of v. 5. And although 'natural' and 'cosmic' are hardly the appropriate biblical categories for the two disasters, there is an intensification there too. Both have to do with the earth and its ability to be fruitful: in the first, this is only temporarily impeded, though that in itself may mean hunger for many and death for some; in the second, the basic resource of the fruitful deeps is removed, and that implies permanent impairment. (It is probable that people supposed that water springs had the same sort of immediate connection with the waters of the abyss under the earth as individual graves had with Sheol, the world of the dead.)

Many intriguing critical questions about these six verses are handled clearly in the commentaries. I mention only one here, and I have already sketched its background. It is vital for their closer interpretation. Have the locusts already finished their task before the visionary interposes? And has the land itself already suffered the fire's worst ravages? The answer to the first question is clearly 'yes' according to the received Hebrew text (MT), which the RSV renders fairly at the beginning of v. 2: 'When they had finished eating the grass of the land, I said . . . '.

The problem in this for many scholars has two roots. The first of these has also two aspects: (a) it is held that the many formal similarities between the first and second visions must extend also to the point at which the visionary speaks; (b) it is maintained that the Hebrew at the end of v. 4 sees the consumption of the arable land as prospective, or at least incomplete. The second root is the belief that we are dealing here with a case of official prophetic intercession: and such activity is pointless once the blow has already fallen.

Very many scholars have found the Hebrew in v. 2 so unusual that it must be wrong; and have adopted Torrey's very simple 'correction' to allow the translation 'when they were finishing eating' or 'when they were about to finish eating'. This is perfectly plausible, and I have long supported it. But there are good reasons for second thoughts. Gese encourages us to read vv. 4-5 in the same way as we must read the MT of v. 2: that the verbal form *w'klh* at the end of v. 4 is not to be understood as 'incomplete', and so a contrast to the immediately preceding *wt'kl* ('ate'/'would eat'), but as co-ordinate in time with the following 'and I said' at the beginning of v. 5.

Of course this reading of the Hebrew makes the 'intercessor' approach rather harder, but not impossible. Forgiveness is a fair request only where life may somehow continue. We must consider later how all the visions relate to reality.

b. Questions of similarity and development are relevant also to the discussion of the second pair of visions, a discussion made all the harder because of the obscurity of the third. The familiar lead plumbline of English and other modern versions is under considerable threat! The third and fourth visions share some formal characteristics a little different from the first and second. The opening, 'Thus he showed me' (for some reason RSV in 7.7 lacks the opening 'Thus' of the Hebrew), is reinforced with the words, 'Amos, what do you see?' (7.8; 8.2). Then, in place of the earlier divine repentance, comes the promise that 'I will never again pass by them'. The difference between the two pairs is not so much that Amos is now involved in his own visions: he had involved himself in the first two. Rather, in visions three and four, he is invited by God to look, and think, and then comment. Apparently, after pondering, he has no come-back.

The finality of the fourth is abruptly expressed in Hebrew quite as terse as the English 'the end has come' (*ba' haqeṣ*). It is regularly held that the point of this fourth scene moves from the visual to the verbal: that what is seen and then named merely provides the occasion for a play on words: from *qayiṣ* (summer) to *qeṣ* (end). The words may even have been pronounced identically in the dialect of the period. A similar interpretation is usually offered of *šaqed* (almond) and *šoqed* (watching) in Jer. 1.11-12. A richer alternative to the interpretation of both visions has recently been argued by Professor Gese.

He notes that just as the almond branch of Jeremiah's vision pushes the blossom directly, before there are any leaves, out of the apparently dead wood when it awakens at the beginning of the season, so it is that action issues from the unlikely source of bare word over which God keeps wakeful watch, and from which divine powers break forth. This is far from mere word-play: it is a symbolic vision *reinforced* by assonance. So too in the case of the basket of summer fruit, where the very basket suggests the *gathering* of the fruit-harvest: harvest with its associations of judgment and of death the reaper. Here too it is what is seen that carries the symbolic meaning, before it is ever put into words. The naming simply underlines, and draws attention to the complementarity of fact and language.

This hint within 8.1-2 at death the harvester allows Gese to argue that v. 3 is integrally related to what has gone before. To death belongs a dirge; and v. 3, at least if 'says the Lord' may be bracketed, is made up of two lines in Hebrew's lament (*qinah*) rhythm.

With this hypothesis secured, what of the troublesome verses in 7.7-9? For all its familiarity, the 'leaden' approach to this vision has always had its difficulties; and in fact it can be traced no earlier than the middle ages. The Hebrew word *'anak* occurs four times in vv. 7-8 (and only there in all of the Hebrew Bible), and has generally been supposed to refer to a lead-weighted (plumb-)line. The most difficult phrase in the Hebrew for this line of approach is the first in which it appears (*homat 'anak*), which must be literally rendered 'wall of lead'. This is usually held (as in RSV) to be a concise phrase for 'a wall built with a plumb line'. Another approach has supposed that the 'lead' had a destructive rather than constructive function: that it provided the tip of a battering ram, rather than a tool for a builder or planner or evaluator.

However since Landsberger's study of 1965, it has been precarious (to say the least) to continue to suppose that biblical *'anak* did in fact mean 'lead'. 'Tin' now appears to be the appropriate metallic equivalent; and that involves shaking again the kaleidoscope of this third vision, for tin belongs neither to the measuring line nor to the demolition process. Professor Gese's discussion is illuminating here too.

Other approaches in recent years have interpreted the 'tin' wall both negatively and positively. On the one side the argument starts either from the softness of the metal and its uselessness in unalloyed form, or from the negative magical meaning of the metal in Mesopotamian rituals. On the other, the case rests on the importance of tin for the production of bronze weapons and the amount of tin available to God symbolized by the wall. Gese himself insists that the phenomena in the visions do preserve their own specific meaning: and it is that meaning which indicates the appropriate spiritual reality. Just as the basket implies gathering, so the wall is not just mass but also military potential. And a metal wall (as opposed to one of stone, wood, or earth) signifies (divine) inconquerability. Then, when God is *seen* standing on such a wall, one assumes it is from the front: as an offensive not a defensive power. For the normal weapon-hard bronze, tin was combined with copper in the proportion 1 : 6. And in fact, roughly in Amos's period, the Assyrian monarch Sennacherib boasted of having increased this proportion of tin (itself ten times more valuable than copper). Accordingly this wall of tin signifies colossal military potential; and the presence in the vision of a further quantity of tin in God's very hand, whether in the form of a weapon or as simple store of available metal, only underscores this.

Two linguistic remarks complete Gese's observations. The first is that *'anak* is the regular word for 'tin' in the Mesopotamian area of Assyrian influence, the normal Hebrew word being *bedil*. The effect of using this foreign import in Amos will be similar to the use in English since the Second World War of 'panzer' divisions to signify *German* armoured formations. It is *Mesopotamian* forces which God is disposing against his people Israel. The second is that the *k* of *'anak* is pronounced between the *ḥ* of *'anaḥ* and the *q* of *'anaq*, both of which signify moaning and groaning. Such an element of wordplay here adds a further dimension to the effectiveness of the third vision, and anticipates the symbolic pun in the fourth.

So much for *'anak*. The other outstanding issue is the relationship of 7.9 to the two preceding verses. Many hold that it was drafted simply as a link to the following narrative in vv. 10-17. However, it can be claimed that, just as 8.3 makes concrete the image of death the reaper or harvester, so too 7.9 removes all doubt that 7.7-8 could point to anything other than the threatening military subjugation of Israel— encapsulated in the centres of religious and royal power and protection. (The 'house' of Jeroboam could refer equally to the royal household or the royal shrine.)

c. With these results achieved, Gese turns to the beginning of chapter

9. Here he finds the third stage and culmination of the series of visions. Its opening is formally different, beginning with the more immediate 'I saw'. Here Amos simply views; he is not himself implicated in the scene, whether as intercessor or under interrogation. (Gese assumes that the commands in v. 1 are addressed not to Amos but to an 'angelic' servant.) There are different layers of meaning again in the image. The blow to the top of the (sanctuary) building will result in a collapse to the very foundations. Yet at the same time the Bethel temple is the head and top-end of the Israelite nation. Once it has been successfully assaulted, the lower parts of the building, the population at large, will be finished off by the sword. Destruction will be total: there will be no escape. This is spelled out in the five 'If' sentences in vv. 2-4a.

Gese's claim that the fifth vision is an original member of the series gains strength, it seems to me, from the presence within it, or at its end, of this further series of five elements, again in the pattern 2 + 2 + 1. The first pair note the absolute polar opposites of 'heaven' and 'hell'; the next the earthly opposites of mountain-top and sea-bed; while the climax in 9.4a approaches historical reality with its dread sword commanded to dog its victims even into captive exile. (As we shall see in future chapters, Gese has noted further five-fold (2 + 2 + 1) structures in the book of Amos.) He suggests that 9.4 once marked the end of the negative and threatening material in the book of Amos. And so when later redaction had further such material to add, it did so in 8.4-14, before the due conclusion and inspired by the catch-word 'end' in 8.2.

2. Vision and Reality

It is one thing to probe the shape and discuss the content of Amos's visions. It is quite another to come to conclusions about their meaning and significance, or indeed even their wider function within the book of Amos. Are they an autobiographical account of private experiences which impelled him on his public course? And, if so, do they *all* precede *any* of his public words, or is his own development mirrored in their progression? Is the public report of these visions in the book a claim to authority? And, if so, are their contents in any sense literal record, or only an expression of a conventional religious code? Indeed is that last question a fairly posed alternative? Were they in fact ever orally proclaimed?

Both Watts and Gordis would persuade us that visions four and five are both subsequent to the initial group of three reported in 7.1-9. Watts in fact believes he has evidence of a two-year timetable of visions corresponding to the '*two years* before the earthquake' of the title verse (1.1).

A more literary account of the matter would find it easy to assume that the presence of these visions at the end of the book does constitute an appended claim to authority: Amos's words deserve attention because of his visions. Most scholars believe that the narrative in 7.10-17 does disturb the original proximity of visions three and four. Its very position there might suggest that its contributor understood the visions as authority-claim. For that story also concerns Amos's right to say what he says. (On the other hand it does not follow that 7.9 was ever publicly proclaimed as seditious utterance.)

Nowhere in the preserved public words of Amos do we find any intercession for his people. Should that warn us against supposing that the visions were experienced in the course of his proclamation? Or is it simply one of several indicators that should remind us that vision operates in a different world from reality, just as dream episodes are different from wakeful experience: by no means completely discontinuous with one another, but different all the same?

The awful fire in the deeps and the wall of tin are manifestly otherworldly, while the locusts and fruit-basket are part of common experience (although they too are symbols for something beyond themselves). This context or backcloth makes all the more acute the question of the fifth vision. It is presented differently; yet quite how is its difference to be described? Is the destruction of *a* sanctuary a symbol for something else, like the removal of access from man to God? Or does the definite article in '*the* altar' (9.1) have a specific sanctuary in mind (presumably Bethel)? If so, then this last vision might be more like the experience of waking out of a dream: a final half-dream in which earlier more exotic images are brought more closely into touch with pressing everyday concerns. The progression within 9.2-4a might suggest that we are on the right track here. For there the last example of attempted escape from the divine destroyer (exile) is more 'realistic' than flight to heaven, hell, or the sea-bed. One aspect of this question we shall leave for a later discussion: if we can be confident that the fifth vision is *both* authentic *and* more immediately 'real', *then* it will be important evidence for the authenticity of Amos's cultic criticism.

There are some other links too between the visions and the contents of Amos 1–6. The book opens with the dread and mysterious words (1.2) which talk of Carmel, and relate the divine voice to dire natural happenings. An unspecified menace attaches to the 'it' which God will not revoke (eight times in the opening two chapters). The image of no escape (9.1b-4a) resumes the same theme from 2.14-16. Again, despite the general other-worldliness of their contents, the visions do share some language with the rest of the book: Jacob (7.2, 5) is the name of the people Amos addresses in 3.13; 6.8 (and also 8.7; 9.8). Imaginative 'seeing' is called for in 3.9 and 6.2; and heightened 'hearing' in 3.13 (and perhaps also in 4.1 and 5.1). The two lines in elegy rhythm that conclude the fourth vision (8.3) are anticipated in 5.1-3; 5.16-17; and also in 5.18ff. and 6.1ff.; while military collapse and exile are dealt with in 4.2-3 and 6.7-8.

One final aspect of Amos's visions deserves mention at this point: their status as religious language, as talk about God. The book of Amos is in fact very sparing in direct prediction about God's acts in the world. A dread 'it' will not be called back. The divine fire will consume the strongholds of Israel's neighbours. 'Cows of Bashan' will be led out in file through the destruction. Leisured revellers will be first into exile. Yahweh's day will be darkness and not light. These are hints and intimations for those who will hear them, but hardly treasonable statements that would stand scrutiny in a duly constituted court—and hardly direct predictions of divine activity that are readily falsifiable.

Amos's visions reinforce this impression of his 'God-talk'. They hint rather than define. They offer images, and only the most summary of statements. They create an impression of dread, rather than deliver a promise and timetable of destruction. If the last vision is relatively clearer, then it corresponds to the culmination of the opening six chapters: 'I am raising against you, O house of Israel, a nation; and they shall oppress you from Lebo Hamath to the Brook of the Arabah'. There too the geographical limits are both polar (north/south) and inclusive. There too the many preceding hints are resumed and made more specific. But only *more* specific. The agent-nation is not named. God has declared; but God is still free.

Further Reading

Supporting and alternative accounts of the five vision reports may be found in the commentaries, especially those mentioned in the Introductory chapter: of Hammershaimb, Mays and Wolff (and, in German, Rudolph).

The issues are also treated in the appropriate handbooks:

Blenkinsopp, *History of Prophecy*, 90-92.
Coote, *Amos*, 15, 53-55, 89-94.
Koch, *Prophets*, 36-44.
von Rad, *OT Theology* II, 50-69, 131-32.

The Hebrew terms for 'seeing' and 'vision' are reviewed in

A.G. Auld, 'Prophets through the Looking Glass: between Writings and Moses', *JSOT* 27 (1983), 3-23 (esp. 10-14).
C.C. Torrey's proposals on the text of Amos 7.2 were made in *JBL* 13 (1894), 61-63.
B. Landsberger's discussion of *'anak* is in 'Tin and Lead: the Adventures of two Vocables', *JNES* 24 (1965), 285-96.

An alternative approach to Amos 7.7-8 by means of textual emendation is reported by

D.L. Petersen, *The Roles of Israel's Prophets* (JSOTS 17), 1981, 77-79.

The biographical approach to the ordering of the visions is argued in

R. Gordis, 'The Composition and Structure of Amos', *HTR* 33 (1940), 239-51.
J.D.W. Watts, *Vision and Prophecy in Amos*, 1958.

A possible intercessory role for Amos is discussed in

W. Brueggemann, 'Amos' Intercessory Formula', *VT* 19 (1969), 385-99.
Petersen, *Roles*, 94.

and, in German, in

Reventlow, *Amt des Propheten* (FRLANT 80), 1962.
E. Würthwein, 'Amos-Studien'.

2

AMOS
A PROPHET?

IF OUR first main discussion has ended up with the likelihood that the report of the five visions *may* be seen as a single composition which *may* go back to Amos, this next topic must take us in a different direction. Just what is our evidence for Amos's *prophetic* credentials? The obvious place to start such a quest is with Amos's response in 7.10-17 to the challenge from the representative of state religion. This is especially convenient because we have already studied the visions, which frame this report. We shall return to scrutinize the 'poem' in 3.3-8, and the summary data in the title verse (1.1).

1. Amos and Amaziah

a. The narrative itself is crafted with considerable skill. It can be usefully viewed as composed of four two-verse sub-units. The first (10-11) sees Amaziah reporting dutifully to his royal master (who is presumably resident some forty miles north of Bethel in Israel's capital Samaria), to whom he quotes Amos's sedition. In the next (12-13), Amaziah warns Amos to leave Israel for Judah, not quoting but hinting at royal displeasure. Amos then responds (14-15) quoting divine authority for his activity in Bethel. And in conclusion (16-17) Amos presses the matter home: he juxtaposes Amaziah's ban on prophecy against the people with Yahweh's dire warning that Amaziah himself will share to the very dregs the bitter cup the whole people must drink.

It is not made clear between vv. 11 and 12 whether Amaziah in fact waited for a reply from the king before proceeding against Amos, or whether he made both moves at the same time, perhaps out of *he claims not to be a prophet*

divided loyalty. Many have given the priest the benefit of the doubt, mainly on the basis of his name (which means 'Yahweh is mighty'), that he was loyal to Yahweh by his own standards; and have held that he sought to protect Amos from the royal wrath he was duty-bound to trigger. However, our proper business is with what the text does seek to tell us, and not with what it leaves untold.

b. All who have worked with this passage recognize that the vexed question of the relationship in time between v. 14 and v. 15 is crucial to this account of Amos's self-understanding. In short, does v. 14 describe Amos's present situation (RSV and NEB: 'I am not a prophet') or his previous state (JB and NEB footnote: 'I was not a prophet')? The problem is rather easier to state than to settle.

Verse 14 in Hebrew makes three statements, but without a single verb. How are we to relate these to the statements about past time made by verbs in v. 15? A famous article by Rowley is widely appealed to for the view that the definite past of the second verse draws the undefined earlier verse into its own time: 'not being a prophet . . . I was taken by the Lord'. Some prestigious scholarly talent has followed him in insisting that plain good sense too demands that Amos is here explaining how his *prophetic* status derives from Yahweh himself.

The following rather literal rendering of v. 14 may give the flavour of the Hebrew: 'Not-a-prophet (am/was) I and not son-of-a-prophet (am/was) I, but-a-herdsman (am/was) I and a-dresser of-sycamore-trees'. English idiom requires the addition of some part of the verb 'to be'. But that verb is much more sparsely used in Hebrew. And so English insists on an interpretative decision on a matter the *actual Hebrew words* leave open. In Hebrew such nominal sentences (sentences without a verb) are reckoned to imply present time unless the *context* demands otherwise. And *that* is the nub of the problem here.

I am much more sympathetic to the position opposed to Rowley's case. This argues (a) that if a single nominal clause normally expresses a temporal present, then a batch of three as here must refer to continuing present time; and (b) that the emphatic opening position of the negative (*Not*-a-prophet . . . I) demonstrates that Amos is bent on *contradicting* Amaziah's assumption that he is a professional prophet, not somehow *reinforcing* it.

I am confident that this is the most straightforward reading of the

Hebrew: any other must be imposed by some sort of exegetical *force majeure*. So far I have just sketched the two main opinions held. Yet another view appeals to a different understanding of the repeated opening Hebrew word, written *l'*. Read as *lo'*, it is simply Hebrew's standard negative, 'not'. But *l'*, it is observed, is also the way that the mark of a strong *affirmation* in the related language of Ugarit would have been written in Hebrew (if in fact this was also known in Hebrew). And Amos 7.14 is held to be part of the evidence for its use in Hebrew. As an argument this is clearly circular; but that is not a fatal criticism if it eases the reading of this passage. However, it seems to me to be precluded by the 'but' in the middle of the verse.

Let us leave for the moment the question of what this short eight-verse text is saying, and turn to the larger question of what it is talking about. The clues to this should come from attending to the wider context of our text. The immediate context within the book of Amos is the series of visions. We have already observed in the last chapter that some few scholars, notably Gordis and Watts, simply take the sequence of material in Amos 7–8 as an indication of the actual chronology of Amos's career. He had three visions about which he had clearly spoken: the end of one of these got him into trouble with the authorities (7.10ff.). Subsequently he had a fourth vision which is reported in the style of the third.

c. For many scholars this represents too naive an approach to the text. In terms of *our* canons of style, this story of Amos and Amaziah seems a rather clumsy interruption of the series of visions, particularly as it sunders the second of two pairs. Even if it is itself deftly drafted, it remains true that it involves a sudden shift from first-person report *by* Amos (in all of the visions) to third-person report *about* him. There is then an immediate *prima facie* case to answer against the originality of this text in its present local context. How far can this be clarified by examining a wider context?

It is here that I find very helpful the article by Professor Ackroyd to which I drew attention in the Introduction. This is not so much because of its conclusions, which I do not find persuasive, and which in any case are very tentatively offered. It is rather because of a novel suggestion he makes while exploring the problem.

Since the work of the great Wellhausen at least, many scholars have sensed some sort of relationship between the second half of Amos 7 and the much longer story in 1 Kings 13 about the man of

God from Judah who challenged Jeroboam I at the very altar of Bethel. The suggestion has usually been that the fuller narrative in Kings, with its several legendary traits, has its origins in the *historical* episode of Amos the Judaean who actually belonged to the time of the later Jeroboam II. The links are certainly impressive: (1) the Judaean connection; (2) the reign of a Jeroboam; (3) confrontation at the altar of Bethel; (4) significant emphasis on 'eating bread'; and we could add (5) the role of the lion who kills the man of God in 1 Kings 13— for lions and roaring are prominent in the wider book of Amos (1.2; 3.4, 8; and 5.20).

The fresh light cast on our text by Professor Ackroyd is his invitation to note the similar links between our eight verses and the even shorter story in 2 Chron. 25.14-16. Here again we are dealing with critique of an Amaziah, though this time King of Judah. Here again we find a prophet accused of meddling in business of state, and warned of the most serious consequences. Here again, after the attempt to silence him, the critic insists on having the last word, which again is a prediction of destruction for the individual who has sought to stand in the way of God's purposes.

We seem to be dealing with too many links between Amos and both Kings and Chronicles for us to dismiss them as coincidental. Even accepting this, it *could* still be the case that Amos's actual encounter with an Amaziah who represented a King Jeroboam has been recorded in the book of Amos, but also half-remembered in different ways which have also been preserved in the books of Kings and Chronicles. It is possible. But three indications make me pause before agreeing. The first we have already noted. This is simply the rather uneasy location of our text in its immediate context. Of course there are links between 7.10-17 and 7.9. But these need not be taken to imply that part of Amos's vision did occasion a meeting with an official. (We have already noted the lack of other obvious evidence that he did in fact proclaim the contents of his visions publicly.) They could also suggest that the presence of 7.9 in the book of Amos was itself the occasion, and provided some of the building-blocks, of a narrative which further explored the nature of Amos's authority. Some of the other 'blocks' were traditions of conflict between divine spokesmen and both Jeroboam and Amaziah.

The second reason is that it seems to me more likely in general that the only story to feature both an Amaziah and a Jeroboam will represent the intersection of two originally separate traditions, rather than the origin of them both. It would be surprising if *both* an original Amaziah disappeared from the version of the story in Kings *and* an original Jeroboam from that in Chronicles. Such a judgment does not *of itself* force one to assume a date for Amos 7.10-17 later than 2 Chron. 25.14ff. (Both our actual texts in 1 Kings 13 and 2 Chron. 25 may be later, developed versions of the traditions which criss-crossed in Amos 7.)

However, my third reason does possibly bear on the question of dating. Seeing a passage from Chronicles as part of the context in which we should read this text from Amos may help to explain the presence in it of the troublesome 'seer' in 7.12. 'Seer' here translates *hozeh*, which with its related nouns and verbs occurs mostly within the Hebrew Bible in one of two situations: in titles of prophetic books (including Amos 1.1); and in material special to the books of Chronicles and not derived from known biblical sources (mostly Samuel and Kings). It is in fact mostly a late-biblical word.

I have to admit that there is at least one counter-indication to this line of argument. That is the presence of the lion executioner in 1 Kings 13. If it is a link with the Amos traditions, it is with the main traditions in that book and not with 7.10-17 in which no animal appears.

d. What I want to suggest now is that attention to this wider biblical context is not simply helpful in establishing the setting and part of the background of what is in a sense a literary 'intruder' in the book of Amos; it may also enable us to control our interpretation of some of its details. I drew attention above to the presence of 'eating bread' in both Amos 7 and 1 Kings 13. If we were to read Amos 7 simply in its own terms, we would naturally follow most commentators in supposing that Amaziah's counsel to Amos to 'flee to the land of Judah and eat bread there' meant (in the context of banning further activity at the shrine in Bethel): 'go and earn your food by giving oracles for hire south of the border'. On the other hand, within 1 Kings 13, 'eat bread' appears to signify 'accept hospitality'. Of course if criss-crossing traditions result in different Amaziahs and different Jeroboams, then they can also involve different meanings of 'eat bread'. However we should at least explore the possibility of a common function and meaning for the phrase. One solution may be that in neither narrative are we dealing with a warning over loss of critical independence, whether by earning one's living or becoming compromised by alien hospitality; and that Amos 7 and 1 Kings 13 simply encourage urgency: 'get across the border into Judah before your next meal'.

2. The Series of Questions in 3.3-8

a. Our preferred translation of Amos 7.14-15 involves us in supposing that for the author of the narrative one did not have to be a 'prophet' in order to receive the divine imperative to 'prophesy'; and indeed that such a command did not turn one into a 'prophet'. Yet our wider discussion of that passage requires us to look further before we suppose this was the view of Amos himself. We may be more likely to find the historical Amos in the balanced poetical rhetoric of 3.3-8, and in particular within vv. 7 and 8 which use both 'prophets' and 'prophesying'.

However, the judgment that Amos 3.3ff. is poetry immediately makes my last sentence problematical. It must be admitted that the principles of Hebrew metre, and indeed the very nature of Hebrew poetry have been hotly debated in recent years. It is equally true that absolute formal regularity within vv. 3-6 can only be achieved by some emendation of the Hebrew text. However, v. 7 is manifestly prose: the structural difference between it and its context is plain.

It is also a fact that the phrase 'his servants the prophets' occurs elsewhere in the Bible only in texts considerably later than the historical Amos. Scholars have normally argued that the phrase is part of 'Deuteronomistic' usage: that is, an element of the terminology of those ancient scholars who edited the books of Joshua to Kings, and perhaps Jeremiah too, in the spirit of the religious ideas at the core of Deuteronomy, scholars who were probably active at the time of the Exile of Jerusalem and Judah in Babylon in the sixth century BCE. I have recently published an argument that even this may be too early a dating for this phrase 'his servants the prophets': we find the formula most often in Jeremiah, in later elements of that book, and in 2 Kings, in additions that appear to be *post*-Deuteronomistic; these pointers to a later dating of the phrase are reinforced by the fact that its other few occurrences are in the later biblical books of Zechariah, Ezra, and Daniel. Amos 3.7, if early, would be the *sole* and striking exception to this pattern.

Objections can be offered to both of these points. It has been urged that there is some rhetorical force in changing tempo (3.7) just before returning to the main theme and pressing home the conclusion (3.8). It is also true that expressions may have been coined long before they became common. And indeed the point is sometimes made that so little Hebrew writing of the biblical period has been preserved for our analysis that such arguments about the history of usage are necessarily fragile. This is good, or at least spirited defence of the received text! But there is a much more serious objection to v. 7 in its immediate context. Far from offering a rhetorical enhancement, it actually appears to do violence to the argument of the whole section.

b. So far we have represented the majority scholarly approach to this passage. But soon the ways divide. Verses 3-6 pose a series of seven rhetorical questions, each expecting the same answer: No! It has been held that they *all* spring from common experience, or at least common belief; and that each testifies to an inevitable bond that links cause to effect. Lions do not roar without prey to protect (a zoologist might quibble: but that is beside the point); traps are not triggered by nothing at all; and a warning horn is not sounded in a town without its people becoming afraid. These are general observations, common to the whole world: there is no special esoteric lore here.

It is widely held that, if we move directly from these questions to v. 8 (that is, ignoring the interpolated v. 7), we find adumbrated there a satisfactory conclusion in its final two questions. The first of these resumes the preceding series by deftly linking the lion roaring (from the beginning of v. 4) with the inevitable fear (from the middle of v. 6). And we are still dealing with universal belief: who ever found himself face to face with a lion without his stomach turning round and his knees shaking? Then the second question presses the conclusion home. So it is with prophesying. *No-one* ever heard the divine voice without prophesying. And the implication is surely there that hearing the divine voice is no more the prerogative of official prophets than fear of wild beasts or air-raid sirens requires special capacities or accreditation.

It is just that strong point which is undercut or neutralized by v. 7 with its class of prophetic servants who are made privy to the Lord's purposes. When we come to v. 8 *after* and so in the light of v. 7, its concluding questions can be read only as testifying to the inevitability of the *prophet's* response to the divine summons and not to the *generality* of this experience. Accordingly we might fairly add our assent to the widespread conclusion that v. 7 is not original to 3.3-8.

We might also concur that v. 8 conceives of *prophesying* being an activity that is not confined to official *prophets*, but open to *anyone* who has heard Lord Yahweh speak. Such a point of view squares with the translation of 7.14 commended above, which has Amos deny that he *is* a prophet, whatever his words and actions may suggest to the contrary. But is even this the original point of the unit under discussion? And is it in fact a unit at all?

A number of reasons have been urged against the originality of v. 3 at the one end and v. 8 at the other. The first of these issues is less relevant to us at this point; however, if we agree to the removal of v. 8 as well as v. 7, then the passage was not about prophesying at all! The arguments marshalled concern both style and content.

Certainly the form of questioning has changed from vv. 3-6: instead of each individual question being introduced by an interrogative marker (*ha-* or *'im*), v. 8 signals its questions with a 'who' in the middle of each element. Equally, the two halves of this verse are shorter than any element in vv. 3-6. Of course in themselves these observations need suggest no more than that the conclusion of the piece is presented differently from the supporting arguments, or, stated rather more deliberately, that the arrival of the conclusion is signalled structurally by a shift in style.

c. Perhaps the more important issue is whether a strong conclusion has not already been reached in v. 6. If that were the case v. 8 might represent a deft re-use of vv. 3-6 to undergird a new point about prophecy even although these verses originally made their own rather different point. This was suggested forcefully over twenty years ago by Smend who drew attention to the fact that vv. 3-6 are in themselves composed of seven elements, a familiar total of completeness. But this conclusion has been tellingly undergirded by a careful and very closely argued scrutiny of Amos 3.3-8 in Lindström's recent discussion of *God and the Origin of Evil*.

The main focus of his attention is v. 6b, which we have so far deliberately ignored. This verse is regularly rendered as in RSV: 'Does evil befall a city, unless the Lord has done it?'. In his book he is concerned to rebut the near-unanimous view of some generations of Old Testament scholars that the Old Testament teaches a doctrine of divine pancausality: that all happenings, good or bad, are to be traced back to Yahweh. This in turn is widely held to have been but a logical consequence of strict monotheism. Where several gods are acknowledged, people's confused perceptions of the world can be attributed to different and even competing deities; but where only one god is recognized, 'the buck stops there'.

Crucial to Lindström's argument is whether Amos 3.6b was in fact a universally recognized truism (at least in Israel) in Amos's day, or whether it was a new point which Amos had to teach by means of the preceding truisms. He offers four arguments for seeing a conclusion in v. 6:

1. The questions in v. 6 are introduced by a different Hebrew word (*'im*) from the interrogative particle used five times in vv. 3-5 (*ha-*). This suggests intensification.
2. The images portrayed in vv. 3-5 belong to *everyday* experience, while that in v. 6a is doubly different: it is less common, and the sequence of cause and effect is reversed. This attracts attention before the decisive question.
3. Intensification can be observed in the metaphors selected: from human concord (v. 3), through subjection of animal by animal (v. 4) and animal by man (v. 5), to violence directed against man (v. 6).
4. Only the final question mentions Yahweh: and this theological orientation makes it a suitable conclusion.

To complement this perceptive account of the four verses, Lindström points to the sustained argument we have not yet discussed in 4.6-11, about the non-recognition of Yahweh by his people despite a series of natural catastrophes. He deduces it was far from an obvious commonplace among Amos's contemporaries that good and bad alike were from God.

If this cumulative strong case is found compelling, then one of two conclusions follows. Either (a) v. 8 is a subsequent development, based on (a partial misunderstanding of) vv. 3-6; or (b) that verse was a once separate fragmentary word of Amos which the editors have preserved alongside other rhetorical questions. Of course in the latter case v. 8 makes the same point as we found earlier in vv. 3-6, 8 as a whole: the *inevitability* of prophesying for *anyone* who has heard Yahweh speak. However, in the former case, we will have learned nothing about *Amos's own* views on prophecy.

d. While Lindström's whole argument with its wide ramifications is very impressive, I think that two counter-factors have at least to be weighed in this matter. One is that the argument in Amos 4.6-11 does not persuade me that Amos had to point out to Israel Yahweh's own hand in their disasters. These verses do blame the people for not responding and returning to Yahweh; yet they leave open the possibility that Israel *knew* what was going on yet *did* nothing about it. The 'recognition' may have been intellectual but not practical.

The other factor concerns the rhetorical structure of the unit in Hebrew. We have already noted above that the questions in v. 6 are differently introduced from those in vv. 3-5. This is all too often camouflaged in English translations, such as those of RSV and JB here. NEB does observe that v. 6 uses *'im* not *ha-*; but it renders *'im* in its conditional sense: 'If a trumpet sounds the alarm, . . . '. I prefer to detect here a striking use of Hebrew alternative *'im* = 'or'; and to suggest that Amos 3.3-6, 8 represents an expansion of a rhetorical device found elsewhere.

Alternative questions introduced by *ha-* / *'im* are often used to establish some common ground in argument on whose basis a new conclusion is drawn. Jeremiah 2 provides two good examples:

> Is Israel a slave? Or is he a homeborn servant?
>> Why then has he become a prey? (v. 14)
> Have I been a wilderness to Israel,
>> or a land of thick darkness?
>> Why then do my people say, . . . ? (v. 31)

In this standard form, the evidence is presented in a double rhetorical question, and then the conclusion is suggested by means of a further question, differently introduced by 'Why?' Given that this is an established rhetorical device, we might be dealing here in Amos 3 with a baroque expansion: instead of one question introduced by the interrogative marker *ha-* we have five (vv. 3-5); instead of its alternate with *'im* we have two questions so introduced (v. 6); and the conclusion of the argument (v. 8) is also presented in two interrogative sentences, with 'who?' at their heart. Let the non-Hebraist beware! As so often, a decision between alternative translations is at the same time a decision between alternative interpretations.

e. We must cut our very long story short. As we saw at the end of c. above, Amos 3.8 appears to deny that 'prophesying' is just the business of 'prophets'. In principle anyone who has heard Yahweh speak can do it. If the verse was uttered by Amos (whether as the culmination of vv. 3-6 or independently of them) then we *have* learned something about his attitudes. But if not (and a good case can be made that vv. 3-6 lead up to a quite different point), then the opinion is someone else's. In that case, just as in 7.10-17, we have not yet acquired evidence for Amos's own attitude to the business of prophecy—unless perhaps an increasingly loud silence! It is of course vital that our reading of the book of Amos should not be prejudiced by anachronistic views about 'prophets'. But I had another reason too for placing this chapter so early in the present volume. A good case can be made for the view that a very large proportion of the book does derive from the words of the historical Amos. After facing some of the most obvious evidence for secondary material in the text, we may be more sympathetic to discussions of authenticity even where the issues are less clear-cut.

Further Reading

Further to the appropriate portions of the already mentioned commentaries and handbooks, the following discussions of Amos 7.10-17 and 3.3-8 are important:

P.R. Ackrodt, 'A Judgment Narrative between Kings and Chronicles? An Approach to Amos 7.9-17', G.W. Coats & B.O. Long (eds.), *Canon and Authority*, 1971, 71-87.

W. Eichrodt, 'Die Vollmacht des Amos', *Beiträge zur alttestamentlichen Theologie* (FS Zimmerli), Göttingen: Vandenhoeck & Ruprecht, 1981, 124-31.

A. Jepsen, 'Gottesmann und Prophet', H.W. Wolff (ed.), *Probleme Biblischer Theologie*, 1971, 171-82.

O. Kaiser, 'Wort des Propheten und Wort Gottes: ein hermeneutischer Versuch', E. Würthwein & O. Kaiser (eds.), *Tradition und Situation*, Göttingen: Vandenhoeck & Ruprecht, 1963, 75-92.

S. Lindström, *God and the Origin of Evil* (Coniectanea Biblica, OT Series 21), 1983, 199-214.

H.H. Rowley, 'Was Amos a Nabi?', *Festschrift Otto Eissfeldt*, Halle: Niemeyer, 1947, 191-98.

H. Schult, 'Amos 7.15a und die Legitimation des Aussenseiters', H.W. Wolff (ed.), *Probleme Biblischer Theologie*, 1971, 462-78.

J.J. Stamm, 'Der Name des Propheten Amos und sein sprachlicher Hintergrund', J.A. Emerton (ed.), *Prophecy* (BZAW 150), 137-42.

J. Wellhausen, *Die Composition des Hexateuchs und der historischen Bücher des Alten Testaments* (2nd edn), Berlin: Georg Reimer, 1889, 280.

The *status quo* challenged by Lindström is conveniently and recently restated in the essay by W. Eichrodt in J.L. Crenshaw (ed.), *Theodicy in the Old Testament*, London: SPCK, 1983, 20.

An alternative translation—and interpretation—of Amos 3.6b has recently been proposed in

M.J. Mulder, 'Ein Vorschlag zur Übersetzung von Amos III 6b', *VT* 34 (1984), 106-108.

I have discussed changes of meaning in the terminology of 'prophecy' in the Hebrew Bible in

A.G. Auld, 'Prophets and Prophecy in Jeremiah and Kings', *ZAW* 96 (1984), 66-82; *idem*, 'Prophets through the Looking Glass', 3-23.

Fundamental recent discussions of the nature of Hebrew poetry include

T. Collins, *Line-Forms in Hebrew Poetry* (Studia Pohl), Rome: Biblical Institute Press, 1978.

J.L. Kugel, *The Idea of Biblical Poetry. Parallelism and its History*, London: Yale University Press, 1981.

W.G.E. Watson, *Classical Hebrew Poetry* (JSOTS 26), 1984 (2nd edn, 1986).

3

WHAT WAS
AMOS?

IT SEEMS appropriate at this point to pause, take stock of our progress so far, and reorientate ourselves. Our first two main chapters have considered evidence for Amos being a visionary or a prophet. Our results have suggested that Amos is not easy to label in these terms.

1. a. On the one side, we do have the report of five visions; and we have reviewed no evidence which compels us to deny these reports to Amos himself. However, these reports in themselves hardly justify our calling Amos a 'seer' (ro'eh), if by that term we mean a 'role label' designating a figure in society who by habit or to order had visions or dreamed dreams and reported their contents as divine revelation. First of all the title ro'eh is not used in the book of Amos (remember that 'seer' in 7.12 translates hozeh). Secondly, scholars are simply making an assumption when they claim that Amos actually reported his visions to his contemporaries, that their contents were part of his proclamation.

The 'evidence' most often cited for this is that Amaziah's complaint of sedition (7.10ff.) 'quotes' the conclusion of the third vision report in 7.9, which accordingly must have been public knowledge. However two counter-observations must immediately be made. (1) Our confidence in 7.10ff. as *historical* record about Amos is now somewhat impaired. (2) Even if not, v. 13 of chapter 7 may point us to a different reading of v. 9. It is regularly supposed that 'Jeroboam shall die by the sword' (v. 11) is a loose quotation of 'I shall rise against the house of Jeroboam with the sword' (v. 9). However 'house of Jeroboam' in v. 9 is the third member of a trio whose first two members are clearly sanctuaries: his 'house' may quite as easily mean his royal *temple* as his royal *household*. And such a reading of v. 9 may lie behind the final phrase of v. 13 which is literally translated '*house* of the kingdom' (not 'temple' as in RSV).

Amos may well have had five visions. And these have been reported to us (ultimately, at least, in writing). But that does not imply that his business was to be a public 'seer'.

b. As for 'prophecy' the situation is similar. The much-cited narrative in chapter 7, as we have just reminded ourselves, is hardly to be considered authentic personal testimony. And even if it was, the most straightforward way to read it is as a denial that he *is* in any sense a prophet, *despite* being sent by the Lord to 'prophesy'. It is possible that 3.8, whether on its own or preceded and reinforced by 3.3-6, may carry us closer to the historical Amos; but it is to an Amos making the same point. We are left to suppose that he may have been critical of and wanted to distance himself from those who were prophets in his own day. Yet no hostility to the prophets is actually reported in the book of Amos, as for example in Isaiah, Micah or Jeremiah— unless it be detected in his '*whoever* would not prophesy?'

2. If we are no longer convinced that either of these labels would have satisfied Amos himself, should we or can we continue the search for a better one? Two texts apparently point to an agricultural background, though we have to note immediately that one of these is the title verse (1.1) which at least in its entirety may not derive from Amos, and the other (7.15) is part of the secondary narrative which has already occupied so much of our attention. However the evidence should at least be briefly reviewed.

The opening words of the title are often confusingly punctuated in English translations: 'The words of Amos who was among the shepherds of Tekoa'. The Hebrew might be better rendered: 'The words of Amos (who was among the shepherds) from Tekoa'. Two points are being made, not one: that he was among the shepherds, and that he was from Tekoa. And the first (now) interrupts the making of the second, hence my proposed brackets. Hebrew would express 'Tekoa's shepherds' a different way (putting the two nouns in construct relationship). The very clumsiness of the Hebrew here suggests that the words I have bracketed are a later supplement. But what do they say?

unique

A *noqed* (1.1) was no ordinary 'shepherd'—the common word is used in Amos 3.12. The only other occurrence of *noqed* in the whole Bible refers to King Mesha of Moab (2 Kgs 3.4), who clearly rears animals in a big way. If that is the actual implication of this rare word, and if it is authentic record, then Amos will have been a man of independent and even comfortable means who did not need to give oracles for hire (cf. 7.15).

We should note in passing that in the ancient Greek translation of the book of Amos (the LXX), in place of the Hebrew *banoqedim* we read *en nakkarim*: that is clearly the transliteration and not the translation of a Hebrew word. But which word? There have been three candidates: (1) *noqed* of the MT (assuming the frequent confusion in Hebrew scripts of *d* and *r*); (2) *'ikkar*, a general word for 'farmer' used in Amos 5.16 (assuming a mistaken duplication of the *n* in *en*); and (3) *boqer*, the word rendered 'herdsman' in Amos 7.14 (a relatively easy confusion of words in Greek: from *en bakkarim* to *en nakkarim*). The second and third suggestions keep Amos in the realm of agriculture, but remove the suggestion of wealth deriving from comparison with King Mesha.

Yet even this comparison has been held to point in another direction. A fragment of evidence from Ugarit lists together *rb khnm* ('chief of priests') and *rb nqdm* ('chief of shepherds'?) as officials of the great temple there. Then, on the assumption that that makes *nqd* a cultic religious figure, and in the knowledge that kings (and so presumably Mesha too) regularly bore cultic responsibility in their realms, Amos has been represented by some scholars as a cultic official (at least before his call). However this is not a compelling use of the Ugaritic evidence. Temples then, like many religious institutions in many societies before and since, were considerable landowners. Their estates presumably required management by officials who need have had no cultic training or responsibility.

Unique, or near-unique expressions dog our quest of the historical Amos! When we turn to 7.14-15, with all our scruples about its authenticity, we find Amos declaring himself a *boqer*. This word is used nowhere else in the Bible (unless just conceivably in the Hebrew text used by the Greek translator of 1.1—see option 3 above). Certainly it can be plausibly related to the common noun *baqar* which refers collectively to (herds of) cattle and other larger domestic animals. Yet is even that not an odd title for someone called from the 'flock' (v. 15) which taken literally would suggest Amos's business was with (smaller) sheep and goats, quite apart from the troublesome *noqed*/'shepherd' of 1.1? Even this talk of a call from following the flock has been thought by some to be a fixed metaphor for elevation from menial to high status. In fact the only other person in the Bible of whom this Hebrew phrase is used is David (2 Sam. 7.8 = 1 Chron. 17.7). Is it mischievous to suggest arguing backwards and propose that the unique 'herdsman' and 'dresser of sycamores' might also be metaphorical? But meaning what?

All of these may be important questions for the interpreter of Amos 7.10-17. Yet the would-be biographer of Amos must remember that, whatever the intent of these expressions, this whole passage is unlikely to derive from Amos himself or any near contemporary. Accordingly they offer no sure guide to how Amos started, or to what he became. They can hardly be taken to clarify his socio-economic status.

3. It seems to me that there is only one way forward. That is to scrutinize those parts of the book which do present themselves as a record of Amos's publicly uttered speeches, for evidence of his standing, his assumptions, and the influences upon him. Their evidence may be more reliable than any we have so far reviewed. Of course as we move now to consider in turn how Israel is set in a wider political and moral context (Amos 1-2), and then Amos's poetical and rhetorical (even perhaps literary?) skill, and his protests against social oppression and religious abuse, our first concern will be with these topics in and for themselves. However it is a quite proper enterprise to sift these materials for any evidence they can offer about the man behind them.

Students of the Old Testament cannot remind themselves often enough that it is only to the books of the Bible themselves that we have direct access. The so-called background information from the fields of history and religion, and indeed language too, to which we often so conveniently appeal as we do our work of interpretation has almost all been culled and reconstructed from these books. Most of it is not hard fact, but only more or less adequate hypothesis. It is from Amos's words that his biography must be produced: it is much too dangerous to operate the other way round, and attempt to clarify his words from 'known facts' about his status—or, even worse, from general theories about prophecy in Israel!

4

HER NEIGHBOURS
AND ISRAEL

AMOS is far from being the only book in the Old Testament prophetic corpus to take an interest in nations external to Israel. But it is remarkable for spotlighting this concern at the very outset. In Isaiah and Ezekiel (and the Greek book of Jeremiah), oracles against the nations appear in the middle of the book; and in Jeremiah (MT) at the end. The tiny book of Obadiah certainly opens with a diatribe against Edom; however, this occupies virtually the whole content of that 'booklet', which is then concluded by a brief positive oracle. When we compare Amos so with its biblical neighbours, we encounter our second structural surprise. The first we noted in Chapter 2: other prophetic books tend to quote vision experiences early and not as here at the end. Simply to note this may serve as a warning not to interpret Amos 1.3–2.3(or 5?) in the light of other biblical books. What then are the more significant issues that have been discussed in connection with these chapters? And what clues are there within Amos 1–2 to guide our evaluation of these issues?

1. Unity and Authenticity

The biggest question is the unity of 1.3–2.16; however, that problem itself has several facets. One is whether or not there is a major break before 2.6ff. That there is an interruption after 2.5 has itself been urged for different reasons.

a. It was Würthwein who argued that the oracles against the surrounding states were formulated before and quite independently of the now parallel critique of Israel. This was to be explained biographically. Amos had begun his career as a 'cultic prophet' responsible for the well-being of his people. Part of his exercise of that responsibility was to call down God's judgment on Israel's enemies. Only after some time, and as a result of his special call by Yahweh (7.14ff.), did he come to recognize that a similar judgment had to be announced against Israel itself. This helps to explain both the similarities (mostly at the very beginning of 2.6ff.) and the differences (especially the very much greater length and detail of the Israel piece) between the two elements of what at first sight appears to be a single composition.

b. On the other side, Coote has claimed recently that priority belongs to the piece about Israel. Its social protest and warning of military disaster represent a perfect example of the historical Amos's utterances. And, in any case, the whole present piece in 1.3–2.16 is too long for the real Amos's terse and direct style.

c. A much greater number of studies have concentrated on another aspect of the unity of these two chapters. This is whether in the original scheme of the unit all seven surrounding nations were considered before the culminating warning about Israel. The negative answer is given in different forms: Judah is regularly excluded, and Tyre and Edom frequently as well. Was Israel's rebuke preceded by a round-up of four, or six, or seven of her neighbours? And yet another oft-discussed issue is whether the whole of 2.6-16 is of a piece, or whether vv. 9-12, or at least 10-12, should be excluded as a secondary 'Deuteronomic' addition.

On all fronts, the arguments disposed concern both form and content. We shall turn our attention first to the outline of the 'literary' shape of 1.3–2.16. As the text stands, the final element on Israel is longer than the others and also concludes in non-standard fashion. That is too plain to require further comment. When the first seven are examined, it can be readily demonstrated that they break down into a sub-group of four (Aram, Philistia, Ammon, and Moab) and another of three (Tyre, Edom, and Judah). The three *lack* the concluding 'says Yahweh' of the four; and also *exchange* their brief complaint and fuller warning of punishment for a longer analysis and more summary warning. These are not points of view, but manifest fact. What is less clear is what we should make of these differences in form. And here the ways divide. For many they are simply acceptable variation within a unified discourse; for as many others they are clearly the first (and most easily documented) token of disunity and supplementation.

A typical defence of the view that only the four are original would go like this. Starting from the formal differentiation just observed it would offer some remarks on the content of each of the sections on Tyre, Edom and Judah. What is said of Tyre in the first part of v. 9b almost exactly repeats the wording in the immediately preceding piece on Philistia (v. 6b). Such repetition is unique within the whole section, and is testimony to a secondary hand at work. Then the 'perpetual wrath' of Edom (v. 11) is held to reflect the deep antipathy between *Judah* (not Israel) and Edom after the latter gloated at the fall of Judah and Jerusalem to the Babylonians at the beginning of the sixth century. Finally the objection lodged against Judah herself (2.4b) is not only less specifically ethical than any of the six that go before it, but is also expressed in terms typical of Deuteronomic thought and later 'Torah-piety'. Questions of content reinforce the doubts already raised by the presence of a formal sub-group within the seven. And of course, just in passing we may note that those scholars who (for good reason or bad!) find 1.3–2.16 too long a composition for Amos's orally delivered communication may be relieved to find grounds for shortening the 'original' piece!

One of the most substantial rebuttals of this 'purging' of the text does in fact go some small distance to meet its arguments. This is in Rudolph's large commentary. He concedes that the final phrases in both 1.11b and 2.4b are short later supplements. That admission removes in two short strokes the clearly post-exilic flavour of the Edom–Judah antipathy, and the Deuteronomic flavour of the protest against Judah's religion. He also insists that we notice the other variations within 1.3–2.5, such as the unique 'kindle' for 'send' in 1.14. These should make less absolute our confidence in the different weight given to exposé or threat, or the presence or absence of 'says the Lord'. As for the different character of the critique of Judah, Amos was after all a Judaean; he may have had no evidence to report of international gross moral turpitude; and in any case, knowing its situation better he was able to go right to the religious heart of her problem. In brief, Rudolph insists that Amos did not schematize. Koch too has urged that close attention to the historical detail of each individual piece justifies the variety in the punishment threatened.

Some middle positions have recently been argued. Christensen and Paul have both claimed that the whole Judah piece must be sacrificed, while those on Tyre and Edom do belong in Amos's composition. Then Cazelles, while accepting the strength of the formal argument for two discrete groups of complaints, in fact claims both the four and the three for Amos himself. He starts from a close rescrutiny of the piece on Tyre in 1.9-10, and in particular its historical location. (1) Assuming that the 'covenant of brothers' (end of v. 9b) refers to a pact with Israel (we know of such formal friendly relations at the time of Solomon and Hiram, and later of Ahab and Jezebel), he observes that elsewhere in the Bible 'covenant' is used only in a theological sense after the exile. (Admittedly he grants Wolff's remark that talk of 'remembering a covenant' is typical of the exilic Priestly stratum of the Pentateuch.) In any case 'Israel' did not exist in the sense that it could contract 'treaties' in the Persian period. (2) He also argues that, while the specific complaint is supposed to be dealing in large-scale slavery, the Hebrew word *galut* strictly means 'exile'. (3) A third part of his platform is to note evidence elsewhere in Amos for activity later than the time of Jeroboam II; he argues that Amos 6.2, like Isa. 10.9, reflects the Syro-Ephraimite War in the later 730s. We know that Tyre became allied to Assyria in 735; and also that in this period Assyrian lieutenants based in Phoenicia had dealings with the Moabite section of Transjordan. Cazelles concludes here that Amos's complaint is against those Phoenician merchants who followed the Assyrian forces into Israel and acted as financial agents in the exiling of her population. Each group of oracles against the nations stems from a different period in his career, and they were only later combined by his disciples.

d. Before we move to consider the integrity of the present version of 2.6-16, two matters might be mentioned that concern the introduction to each one of the eight pieces. One is the near-unanimity of the view that the 'for three . . . and for four' formula is indebted to the language of wisdom. Terrien and Wolff have been foremost in advancing the claim that we can find many points of contact between Amos and the wisdom tradition in Israel: and even their critics admit that at least here they have a good case.

The other matter is the identity of the mysterious 'it' which Yahweh will not revoke. Wolff has claimed that Yahweh's *word* is meant. Many have held that the phrase is deliberately and menacingly ambiguous. Against both these approaches, Knierim has collected an impressive amount of evidence to justify the view that the first hearers of this phrase would have discerned in it reference to Yahweh's '(burning) wrath'. (His case however has not impressed Gese, who holds to the menace of ambiguity.)

2. **The Final Oracle**

The final oracle uses against Israel exactly the same formula as has opened the previous seven; and, like the others, it moves immediately to detailed critique. However there are two differences in the complaints. The wrongs are no longer national and military but domestic and social; and the catalogue is longer. Then there is no parallel at all to the middle section (vv. 9-12) which underscores the scandal by recalling specific moments in Yahweh's provision for Israel. And finally the punishment is not expressed in the formulaic sending of fire, but in obscure language about an (over-)full cart (v. 13) and a disaster from which none but the mightiest hero will escape, and that barely (vv. 14-16)!

It is the middle section, however precisely defined, on which most discussion of the integrity of the passage has focused. Mays introduces the discussion very well. He notes on the one side the force of the suggestion that vv. 10-12 could have expanded the theme of v. 9, while anticipating the second-person plural address of v. 13. On the other side, against the commonly advanced observation that these middle verses are couched in familiar (and even Deuteronomic) language, he cautions that established terminology is to be expected in such recitation. Blenkinsopp is influenced by the fact that the historical reproach breaks the usually immediate link in the book of Amos between indictment (vv. 6-8) and verdict (vv. 13-16). Similarly, Coote finds vv. 9-12 to be a B-stage insert into an A-stage composition, an insert already prepared for by the addition of 'by every altar' and 'in the house of their god' in v. 8. Then Petersen, while himself impressed by the force of the argument that vv. 10-12 are a Deuteronomic insert, concedes that if one were 'constrained' to argue for the integrity of the whole, the thrust of the piece *could* be described as Amos's protest against the wrong treatment of certain classes of Yahwist.

Koch's large earlier study lists many useful pros and cons in the backward and forward argument over the 'Deuteronomic' character of the disputed verses. Most usefully, it seems to me, he reminds us of Bentzen's earlier contribution to this issue. Bentzen had been the first to advance the case in connection with the oracles against the other nations that they resembled the Egyptian execration texts, in which foreign nations on the periphery were cursed in a more or less fixed geographical order to Egypt's benefit. He also observed that Ps. 81.7-9 (English vv. 6-8) may provide a ritual parallel within the Old Testament to this sort of historical review associated with divine rebuke:

> I relieved your shoulder of the burden;
> > your hands were freed from the basket.
> In distress you called, and I delivered you;
> > I answered you in the secret places of thunder;
> > I tested you at the waters of Meribah.
> Hear, O my people, while I admonish you!
> > O Israel, if you would but listen to me!

And that reminder may serve as a convenient introduction to a short review of the purpose of the whole composition.

3. Gese and Barton

The foremost recent discussions seem to me to be Barton's short monograph on 1.3 to 2.3, and Gese's already mentioned article on composition in Amos. There is an interesting convergence in these studies published in 1980 and 1981, and so quite independent of each other.

a. Gese opens with the insistence that the clear differences between the group of four and that of three demand explanation; and that it is insufficient simply to hold that the smaller group *could* be authentic. Even the two attempts mentioned above to preserve Tyre and Edom while sacrificing Judah are a failure. The five remaining authentic oracles exhibit the same $2 + 2 + 1$ schema detected in the vision-reports. Aram and Philistia are paired as Israel's archetypal enemies (this is reflected also in Isa. 9.11). The link between Ammon and Moab is geographical and genealogical. The offences too are of different character: rules of war are at stake in the first pair; sacral law in the second. It is only when we reach the Israel climax that the four crimes promised in the standing opening formula are listed in full: vv. 6b, 7a, 7b and 8. These should not be misread for seven complaints: three of them are expressed in parallelism from two aspects. The four wrongs are again a pair of pairs, civil and sacral. And this correspondence between Israel's four-fold guilt and the guilt of her four neighbours makes Israel's blame all the more impossible to deny. Brilliantly Gese notes that 2.14-16 forms a matching coda like 9.2-4. Of the would-be escapees, a first pair are foot-soldiers, a second are mounted, while the fifth is the mighty hero who just makes it away. (He accepts the widespread view that v. 14b and v. 15ab are additions.)

Gese does not insist that such five-part structures go back to Amos himself. His concern is with patterns detectable in the Book of Amos. But the presumption is naturally there to be further explored. These and other aspects of composition in the book are the business of our next chapter.

b. But first an account of Barton's distinctive monograph. He too believes that only four 'oracles are authentic words of the prophet' and 'that the Judah oracle is certainly, the Edom oracle almost certainly, and the Tyre oracle very probably, not by Amos'. The conclusions to which he is arguing are helpfully summarized at the outset. The condemnations of the other nations are meant with full seriousness, and intend to arouse in Amos's hearers a sense of moral outrage. 'Having won the people's sympathy and agreement, he rounds on them by proclaiming judgment on Israel too.' His technique both ensures a hearing and makes it harder for his audience to exculpate themselves.

'For Amos to have supposed that this technique would be successful, he must have held the following beliefs about his intended audience's mentality:

1. That they thought manifest evil-doing both deserved and would receive divine punishment.
2. That they regarded the nations condemned as moral agents, i.e. as answerable for their actions, particularly in the conduct of war.
3. That they thought Israel had a specially privileged position which indemnified her against divine judgment.
4. That they did not expect prophets to proclaim judgment on Israel.
5. That they did not regard the kind of sins of which Amos accuses Israel as at all comparable in gravity with atrocities in war.

6. That it was more obvious to them that the nations had moral obligations toward each other than that Israelites had moral obligations among themselves.'

On the basis of this analysis he deduces that Amos was not being original in his claim that foreign nations were subject to moral obligations. Then, if this was a consensus position, we shall not be likely to discover its underlying rationale. Where Barton does locate Amos's originality is 'in two things: (i) in regarding social morality as a decisive area of conduct, just as important for the continuance of Yahweh's favour as the avoidance of much crasser and more 'obvious' crimes; and (ii) in arguing with the people so as to show that their conduct is unreasonable and their complacency foolish and shortsighted'.

Further Reading

Again the standard commentaries are a prime resource, as too the handbooks already cited:

Blenkinsopp, *History of Prophecy*, 88-89, 96.
Coote, *Amos*, 11-12, 32-36, 58-59, 66-73.
Koch, *Prophets*, 44-50, 66-69.
Petersen, *Roles*, 60-62.

Important earlier discussions of these chapters are

A. Bentzen, 'The Ritual Background of Amos 1,2–2,16', *OTS* 8 (1950), 85-99.
S. Paul, 'Amos 1,3–2,3: A Concatenous Literary Pattern', *JBL* 90 (1971), 397-403.

Recent discussion of the opening two chapters of Amos has been considerably enhanced by

Gese's 'Komposition bei Amos', esp. 86-93

and the very readable short monograph

J. Barton, *Amos's Oracles against the Nations* (SOTS Monograph Series 6), CUP, 1980.

The interesting proposal that some of the 'lapses' from regularity in the formulae of Amos 1–2 may have been a deliberate device to control scribal accuracy is made in

S. Segert, 'A Controlling Device for Copying Stereotype Passages? (Amos i 3–ii 8, vi 1-6)', *VT* 34 (1984), 481-82.

The case for the two main stages in the edition of Amos 1–2 being much closer than regularly supposed is ably put in

> H. Cazelles, 'L'Arrière-Plan Historique d'Amos 1,9-10', *Proceedings of the Sixth World Congress of Jewish Studies* Vol. I, Jerusalem: World Union of Jewish Studies, 1977, 71-76.

The attempt to define the mysterious 'it' involves a useful review of much of the content of the chapters in

> R.P. Knierim, '"I will not cause it to return" in Amos 1 and 2', G.W. Coats & B.O. Long (eds.), *Canon and Authority*, 163-75.

5

LITERARY
ISSUES

IT IS convenient to start exactly where we left off in the previous chapter, with Professor Gese. He has rendered it plausible that in chapters 1–2, as in 7–9, we are dealing with an original five-part structure which has been secondarily expanded. He draws attention to one other such 5-element pattern in this book: in 4.6-12. No commentator doubts that we have here the report of five plagues punctuated by a standard refrain. However, Gese is unable to agree with Mays (p. 78) that 'there is no perceptible development in the section'. He suggests rather that the first pair deals with lack of food and water; these are the simplest form of catastrophe, and thirst is worse than hunger. Disease of vegetation and human plague are the next more terrible pair: now it is not just deficiency, but malign external influence. The climax is a catastrophe commensurate with the divine overthrow of Sodom and Gomorrah. Gese himself does not develop further the implications of his triple discovery. However, it is immediately clear that it both demands and enables a new approach to the issue of 'composition in Amos'. I note immediately that each of his passages is from a different 'section' of the book of Amos. May it be that those divisions of the book which we can now so clearly detect (1–2 / 3–6 / 7–9) owe more to later editorial decisions than to distinct source materials? However, before we proceed with such larger questions, it will be useful first to review more of the book, and particularly materials that immediately raise issues of literary structure.

1. The Structure of Amos 5.1-17

Commentators and translators have long had difficulty with elements of 5.1-17. It is hardly an oversimplification to claim that these have focused on the problem of what to do with v. 7. It is not very easy, though possible, to handle it as a single independent verse-unit. It is no easier to see it as the conclusion of vv. 4–6 or as the beginning of vv. 8-9. Many have felt it is a dislocated fragment; and some translations have even proposed its relocation. However some recent studies of the whole passage have apparently solved this old problem with a novel approach to its context.

a. De Waard was the first to argue persuasively that Amos 5.1-17 is an example of palistrophe—this Greek term simply indicates that the passage turns back on itself. To the introductory elegy (A) corresponds the concluding summons to mourn (A'); to the invitation to 'seek me and live' (B) corresponds the similar one to 'seek good and not evil' (B'); the troublesome complaint in v. 7 (C) corresponds to similar protest three verses later (C'); and alone at the hinge point of these two panels is the 'doxology' (D). This gives the pattern

```
A (1-3)                                          A' (16-17)
      B (4-6)                            B' (14-15)
            C (7)          C' (10-13)
                  D (8-9)
```

A further refinement to this basic suggestion solves the problem of v. 7, which drew our attention to wider issues at stake in the chapter as a whole. De Waard observes that in the hinge or keystone section, the 'doxology', an inversion has occurred: the apparently strategic words 'Yahweh is his name', which conclude the similar 4.13 and 9.5-6, appear in the *middle* of 5.8-9—the hinge is also constructed of a tiny pair of hinged panels. If such mild 'violence' to the normal pattern of 'doxologies' is possible, the dislocation of v. 7 is more readily understood as deliberate.

This is already an attractive approach to seventeen often difficult verses; but it is further commended by de Waard's observation that vv. 4-6 are themselves palistrophic. This microcosm, this panel-structure in a nutshell, invites us by its very (second) position in the composition to pay attention to the pattern of the whole and to be open to detecting that larger example of the pattern of which it is itself a part.

Immediately the question must be raised whether such a rhetorical structure could have been appreciated by the ear, or whether its complexity demands that we interpret it as a stage in the literary re-formation of Amos's words in the familiar book. In his brief endorsement of de Waard's argument, Coote is quite clear that the latter is the case.

b. Tromp too has followed de Waard's lead, and offered a thorough account of these verses in a wider rhetorical context, as the embodi-ment of a highly sophisticated attempt at communication. He also is in no doubt that the whole composition is secondary. This is immediately clear from the 'lengthy and prosaic sentence' in v. 1 'which stylistically does not match the following poem'. He proposes a rather different analysis of the core of the composition to de Waard's C–D–C' (vv. 7-13):

A (v. 7):	accusation	1 line
B (vv. 8-9):	doxology	4 lines
A' (v. 10):	accusation	1 line
C (vv. 11-12a):	threat	4 lines
A" (v. 12b):	accusation	1 line
(D [v. 13]:	general conclusion?)	

Such a structure suggests connections to its readers, but leaves them with the responsibility, even the need, to work at the text themselves. The use of the doxology is paradoxical: 'concealing the utterance of thought which is important but dangerous in the concrete situation behind an utterance which seems to be harmless'. To turn from accusation to praise appears to be a move to the less dangerous, until after repeated accusation it is clear that the invoca-tion of God simply underscores the threat. (We have to remember the evidence in the story of the unfortunate Achan [Josh. 7.19] that doxology could be required before capital sentence was executed.)

Tromp goes on to demonstrate beyond reasonable doubt that the seventeen verses constitute a deliberate unit. What is already suggested by the basic palistrophe with the subtle balance at its core is made all the plainer by his analyses of divine appellatives; and of alternation between first and third person in mention of Yahweh, and between second and third with reference to those addressed (second being used effectively for repeated appeals); and even of sound patterns in the Hebrew.

When first confronted with de Waard's evidence for palistrophic structure in 5.1-17 the student may be impressed by the biblical author's artifice. After working through Tromp's development of the issues, it is hard not to be convinced of the artistry of the unit rather than of its artificiality. We are not dealing with originally cohesive sub-units wrenched apart and forcibly reassembled, jagged edges and all. What links the sub-units is as clear as what divides them. Two examples will suffice as illustration. Verse 3 ends the first part and v. 4 begins the next; yet each opens the same way. The accusation in v. 7 is manifestly distinct from the 'doxology' in vv. 8-9; yet Israel and Yahweh are compared and contrasted in their ability to 'turn' one thing into its opposite: right into poison, or darkness into morning.

Tromp addresses himself only briefly to the issue of Amos's own contribution to the stuff of the passage. The laments at beginning and end will be his, but not their connection—each is self-supporting. 'As to the reproaches and proclamation of judgment in vv. 7.10-13 there is no compelling reason to deny them to Amos.' The issue of the doxology he does not pronounce about, merely noting that it belongs with the others in the book. 'The crucial question arises with the exhortations' in vv. 4-6 and 14-15. If Amos is simply a prophet of doom they cannot be his; and so the present composition cannot even substantially be his. He argues attractively that Amos was not simply a morbid orator who delivered 'a desperate message . . . to those irrevocably doomed to death and destruction'. Rather he 'is trying to persuade the others that something radical must be done, by impressing upon them the disastrous consequences of their present conduct'. The clash of a *dirge* for *virgin* Israel will have been particularly effective.

Tromp appears to me to have made very plausible *both* that most of the material in 5.1-17 originates with Amos *and* that the artistic composition represented by this passage is essentially literary, probably the result of several drafts, and so almost certainly not by Amos. He seems not yet to have been aware of Gese's work. Has he given us any clues to how *we* might re-evaluate that?

c. Overlapping territory is also mapped by Lust in an article submitted for publication in 1976 before de Waard's work was available, yet only published in 1981 and not noted by Tromp. His principal concern is with Amos 5.4-6 and 14-15; and we shall return in a later chapter to his view that the former belongs to the move in Josiah's time to centralize the cult, while the latter is even later and Deuteronomistic. What is worth reporting here is the scheme he proposes in a closing footnote for the composition of the wider context of these passages:

iv 1-3	against the women of Samaria
iv 4-5	against the cult
iv 6-12	announcement of judgment
v 1-3	funeral lament
v 4-6	exhortation 'seek Yahweh'
v 7.10-12	against corruption in the courts
v 14-15	exhortation 'seek good'
v 16-17	wailing in the streets
v 18-20	the judgment: the Day of the Lord
v 21-27	against the cult
vi 1-7	against the men of Samaria.

2. Composition according to the Commentaries

Such attempts as we have so far reviewed to probe the coherence of larger editorial sub-units of the book of Amos are a relatively recent scholarly concern; and so they are barely reflected in the standard introductions and commentaries.

a. Hammershaimb simply notes that 'the want of an ordered plan to the book suggests that it was not put together by Amos himself but by others, possibly by his own disciples'. But he insists that this does not 'affect the genuineness of the sayings'.

b. Mays is very complimentary about Amos's art. In fact he anticipates Gese's interest when he finds this 'most apparent in the three composite sayings' (oracles against the nations, recitation of ineffective curses, and vision reports) in which he 'creates a sequence of increasing emphasis and urgency that builds to a climax'. As to the book itself, 'true to its title' it begins with a large block of sayings (1.3–6.14). Most can be confidently attributed to Amos; but the final form of the book 'was the result of a process of formulation which reached from Amos down at least into the exilic period'.

c. Rudolph takes the assumed core of the title verse (1.1) as his point of departure: the section of the book which best fits 'The words of Amos . . . two years before the earthquake' is the immediately following and well-constructed Amos 1–2. His disciples had been involved in the publication of the several other less ordered sections; and the closing positive oracle (9.11-15) had never been uttered orally, but was first made public in its written form.

d. Wolff had already suggested that the 'core' of the title (for him simply 'The words of Amos from Tekoa') had first introduced what is now just one section of the book; for Wolff that is the collection of sayings in chapters 3–6. Amos 1–2 is disqualified by being introduced as Yahweh's words. These sayings in fact represent the first of six discrete layers of material in the present book. Next come the two five-part series which also stem from Amos: the oracles against the nations, and the visions. There follow the early Amos school; the Bethel-interpretation of the period of Josiah; the Deuteronomistic redaction; and finally the post-exilic salvation eschatology.

e. As already noted, Coote is very sympathetic to Wolff's position. He insists that his own method of reducing 'the composition of the book of Amos to a three-stage process is an oversimplification' proper to an introductory essay.

3. **Morgenstern and Koch**

a. Until the recent cooperative project led by Koch, the most lengthy published studies of Amos must have been those of Julius Morgenstern: the first three parts published in the 1930s, and the last one posthumously thirty years later. His conviction was that Amos gave but one connected sermon, at the Bethel sanctuary. Our inherited book gives an extremely imperfect account of this performance: not only has the text been seriously dislocated, but much secondary material has been added to the sundered fragments.

In his view this sermon began with the four authentic oracles against the nations. The following arraignment of Israel itself is made up largely of 2.6-8; 4.4-12; 5.4-5; 5.21-24. After a 'transition' garnered from here, there and everywhere, there follow six almost as composite denunciations, culminating in the 'doom of Israel' recomposed from materials in 6.8; 7.9; 5.26-27. Morgenstern's collage is quite an impressive Hebrew speech '*after* Amos'! But it seems to require an almost fevered imagination to draw plausible lines of development from his baroque hypothesis to the book of Amos we know and have to deal with.

This quest for a larger coherent basic unit could just be portrayed as a precursor of the contemporary interest in more extended rhetorical patterns; yet it can barely co-exist with the lingering dominant conviction that Amos as oral performer uttered quite short oracles. Coote for example insists on this strongly as he reconstructs his basic A-stratum.

b. The proposals of the 'cooperative' led by Professor Koch tend in a different direction. In passing it should be noted that for all its attempt at comprehensiveness, it seems a remarkably isolated work. The admirable commentaries by Hammershaimb and Mays are nowhere referred to. Equally I have found hardly a reference to this large study in works prepared since its publication in 1976. It is also a little disappointing for English readers that no summary of the literary-critical results of this project is offered in the Amos chapter of Koch's *Prophets of the Assyrian Period*.

Koch's team arrives at four main sections in Amos: 1–2; 3–4; 5.1–9.6; 9.7-15. Each of the chapters in the second is a meaningful sub-section. And there are six such sub-units in the long third section: 5.1-8; 5.(7)9-17; 5.18-27; 6.1-14; 7.1–8.3; 8.4–9.6. When defining both main sections and sub-sections this study pays close attention to introductory and concluding formulae. This in itself is not new. J. Lindblom had insisted in *Prophecy in Ancient Israel* (1962), in his own discussion of the 'coherent revelation' within chapter 5 'that begins with a woe-cry in v. 18 and ends with the oracle-formula "says Yahweh" (v. 27), that it would be entirely out of accord with the methods of the collector of the sayings of Amos if vv. 21-27 should be separated from vv. 18-20, so that we had to do with two separate revelations instead of one. Had the collector regarded the passages in question as two independent utterances, he would without doubt have marked the end of the former or the beginning of the latter by an oracle formula or another word or expression such as he used to separate different sayings from each other' (p. 317).

4. Comment

A thorough review and discussion of Koch's major project is

impossible in this compass. I can only express some immediate doubts. Firstly, I find no sufficient account of why some of the introductory or concluding formulae in the book of Amos are held to do double duty: as marking the beginning or end of both a major unit and a sub-unit. Then, it requires demonstration that the connections and separations 'suggested' by such formulae do correspond to Amos's own intentions and not just to the attitudes of his editors. A number of very plausible recent accounts of the redaction of various biblical books have suggested that some clearly marked divisions in the inherited text represent very late editorial decisions. In books like Jeremiah and Joshua, where we are lucky to have inherited quite different editions from ancient times, it is often precisely because of such late interpolations in one tradition or the other that the Hebrew text (MT) differs from the Greek (LXX).

There is just a little evidence of the same phenomenon in the book of Amos, although in the main the ancient versions of Amos attest the same text of the book as the familiar Hebrew. Greek witnesses 'lack' mention of the phrase 'oracle of Yahweh God of Hosts' in 6.8 and 6.14, and some of these are also without the shorter 'oracle of Yahweh' in 3.10. I would handle this evidence differently from Koch. The presence or absence of these formulae is all the more significant because there are in fact very few such pluses and minuses in our evidence for the text of Amos. It makes me question the adequacy of the Koch criteria, when I find that these textual divergences are simply noted in his work, yet with no discussion of their implications. The presence of the formulae in the Hebrew text is simply treated as a significant and original marker of sub-units of text.

To recapitulate: I have little doubt that (the addition of) such formulae had editorial significance. What does concern me is the suggestion that the editorial procedures being noticed were devised to take account of and to demonstrate recognition of breaks in the text inherited by these editors from Amos. If we have good textual evidence that some of these markers (like the three mentioned above) were introduced quite late, we must at least ask ourselves how many more were added much later than the activity of Amos and his close circle, even when we have no such evidence.

It seems to me too that Koch's work is vulnerable to some of the implications of the studies of de Waard and Tromp. The Hamburg project treated the doxologies as subsequent to Amos's own activity, and at least those in 4.13 and 9.5-6 as markers of the end of major sections of the present book. (In other prophetic books too, doxological materials such as the closing verses of Jeremiah 10 and all of Isaiah 12 round off large blocks of text, and may just be evidence of very early liturgical handling of 'canonical' texts.) The fact that de Waard sees (the inverted) 5.8-9 as the single focus of 5.1-17 and Tromp portrays it no less significantly as the paradoxical balance of the threat in vv. 11-12a should make us reconsider whether 4.13 and 9.5-6 are simply pious conclusions of the five-element compositions Gese has studied. If not actually contributed by their author, they are certainly appropriately placed.

Gese's work also makes me ask a question about the independence of Koch's four main sections of the book of Amos. His second, third and fourth begin at 3.1, 5.1 and 9.7. Yet we should notice that, just as after the opening chapters and after the visions the question of Israel and people of God is *explicitly* raised (3.1-2 and 9.7), so too the third five-part composition in 4.6ff. and doxology lead immediately into the dirge for virgin Israel, which *implicitly* portrays the demise of the nation. In each case we may be dealing not with the end of a literary section, but rather with the climax of an argument whose conclusion is then immediately drawn.

The last word is far from having been said on the literary structure of the book of Amos. But important steps towards this goal have been taken. And as these are further evaluated, conclusions may become appropriate concerning the activity of Amos himself.

Further Reading

The fundamental studies on the composition and structure of Amos 5 appear to be a Benelux preserve:

J. de Waard, 'The Chiastic Structure of Amos V,1-17', *VT* 27 (1977), 170-77.

J. Lust, 'Remarks on the Redaction of Amos V4-6,14-15', *OTS* 21 (1981), 129-54.

N.J. Tromp, 'Amos V 1-17: Towards a Stylistic and Rhetorical Analysis', *OTS* 23 (1984), 65-85.

However, a rather similar approach is carried out on a larger scale in

W.A. Smalley, 'Recursion Patterns and the Sectioning of Amos', *The Bible Translator*, 30 (1979), 118-27.

Rhetorical analysis of a chapter not regularly deemed a single unit is found in

> Y. Gitay, 'A Study of Amos's Art of Speech: A Rhetorical Analysis of Amos 3.1-15', *CBQ* 42 (1980), 293-309.

The first three parts of J. Morgenstern's extensive 'Amos Studies' were published in *HUCA* 11 (1936), 19-140; 12-13 (1937-38), 1-53; 15 (1940), 59-304; and the last in *HUCA* 32 (1961), 295-350.

There is a wealth of suggestive comment in Coote's *Amos among the Prophets* (1981), whose sub-title is 'Composition and Theology'. He admits that he is depending on the work of Wolff whose results he is also schematizing and simplifying. Coote outlines three main literary stages: his Stage A represents the work of the prophet Amos himself; Stage B describes 'how the words of Amos were reactualized in the seventh century' and is titled 'Justice and the Scribe'; Stage C concerns 'Exile and Beyond'.

The pioneering study in this territory was

> W.H. Schmidt, 'Die deuteronomistische Redaktion des Amosbuches. Zu den theologischen Unterschieden zwischen dem Prophetenwort und seinem Sammler', *ZAW* 77 (1965), 168-93.

His approach was further developed in Wolff's large-scale commentary, but heavily criticized in that of Rudolph.

Discussion of many of these issues in the rather wider context of a process of reactualization, or re-reading, or what was called first in French 'relecture', within the prophetic literature, is handled in

> J. Vermeylen, *Du Prophète Isaïe à l'Apocalyptique* II, Paris: Gabalda, 1978 (pp. 519-69 deal with the book of Amos).

A defence of the conservative view that the book is a substantial unity and the work of Amos himself can be found in

> R. Gordis, 'The Composition and Structure of Amos', *Poets, Prophets and Sages: Essays in Biblical Interpretation*, London: Indiana University Press, 1971, 217-29.

Koch's 4-part structure is criticized also by

> A. van der Wal, 'The Structure of Amos', *JSOT* 26 (1983), 107-13—he proposes the simple 2-part structure: 1–6 // 7–9.

6

SOCIAL AND
RELIGIOUS CRITIQUE

IT WOULD SEEM tidy at first to handle in separate chapters Amos's criticism of society and of cult. Certainly for many readers of the book these are quite distinct matters, although with some area of overlap. And these readers may well be right. However some have long held that the two topics are inextricably linked. Accordingly it seems to me that we must proceed with some caution, and divide the matter rather differently: first gathering and offering preliminary comment on the relevant texts, to explore what they say (at least on the surface), and then returning to the material to reconsider what they may actually be talking about.

In fact, to list the texts is already to suggest the inter-relatedness of the two topics. The principal portions concerned with social matters are: Amos 2.6-8; 3.9-11, 13-15; 4.1-3; 5.7, 10-13; 6.1-8, 11-12; 8.4-7; however, in the very first of these, 2.8 draws attention to altar and house of God as the significant locale of Israel's misdemeanours. Then cultic issues are to the fore in Amos 4.4-5; 5.4-6, 14-15, 21-27; and possibly 8.9-10 as well; but social issues are never far distant from these texts.

1. Texts

There is no need here to offer detailed commentary on the individual *ethical issues* which Amos addresses. That is very acceptably provided in the commentaries. But it is worth drawing attention to two matters.

a. The first is that there is widespread agreement that the first set of passages listed above are all from Amos himself. Coote, in the service of his 3-stage reconstruction of the development of the text of Amos, makes a small but significant deviation from this judgment. He holds that the mention of altar and house of God in 2.8 is secondary: from his stage B, and not from the original authentic stage A.

b. A little more requires to be said about the second. As already pointed out in connection with the oracles against the nations in chapters 1 and 2, there is a 'superlative' or exaggerated quality to Amos's critique. He so states his criticisms that it is well-nigh impossible to answer him back, as the following examples will illustrate,

(1) It is clear from the outset in *2.6-8* that the defaulting debtor is more 'in the *right*' for Amos than those who prosecute him and sell him into slavery, however legal their procedures, since 'righteous' (or 'just') is strategically placed earlier in the line than 'poor'. Then in the next line our sympathy is engaged by the verb $\check{s}'p$, which is even stronger than our 'walk over'. Unless Coote is right about the two mentions of locality being additional, the temperature of the already hot water is raised by mention of the insult done to 'my holy name'. (The phrase might also be translated 'the name—or reputation—of my holy place'.) And finally, as if the deeds themselves, or the terms in which they have been described, are not enough, v. 9 reminds us that Yahweh is no static holder of a sacred place but has from ancient times been an active benefactor of Israel, and is now ill-repaid by the behaviour of that people.

(2) The exaggeration in *chapter 3* is of a different sort. Verses 9-11 summon up in our imagination the filling of the vast natural amphitheatre round hill-top Samaria by crowds from distant Philistia and even more distant Egypt. These crowds will readily witness Israel's crimes, so enormous are they: whole treasuries packed with violence and destruction. This image half fades and is replaced in v. 11 with the foreign visitors now an enemy surrounding the land and plundering the ill-gotten gains. Before we leave chapter 3 we note in passing that vv. 14-15 link religion and society, altar and luxury, in their threat of doom.

(3) *Amos 4.1-3* singles out Samaria's leading women for special mention. These fine fat cows tyrannize the weak and the poor—and even their husbands, who should be their 'lords and masters' yet are at their beck and call to finance their rich living. They will soon be prodded and goaded into a more respectful cattle-file: as captives bound for exile.

(4) The artfully dislocated *5.7* (recall our discussion in the last chapter) deftly reminds us, with its talk of right(eousness) itself cast to the ground, of those in the right who were trampled over in 2.6-8. Then, while 2.6 was content to introduce three revolts of Israel or four, *5.12* brands the examples of rebellion as 'numerous and mighty'.

(5) The first half of *Amos* 6 is a skilfully composed unit. Those who have been most prominently at ease (v. 1) will be equally prominent in the queue of exiles (v. 7). In this quick review I want to pause only over two points. Despite the almost proverbial familiarity of 'put off the evil day' in v. 3a, I venture another translation as closer to the grammar of the Hebrew and an appropriate anticipation of the second half of the verse. The whole would read:

> 'You who defer evil to the day—
> you have advanced the enthronement of violence.'

The point would be that evil is usually practised in dark secret. Only the most confidently wicked choose daylight for their activities: and their success is a harbinger of the day when evil will openly assume power.

Then it is important to draw attention to the scandal lurking in v. 6. It is hard to suggest the flavour of the Hebrew words in anything short of an unliterary over-pedantic rendering: but the Hebrew would have sent a frisson of horror up the spine of its first hearers. (a) The 'bowls' from which they drink wine are cultic sprinklers. (b) The 'first' of the oil should have been strictly reserved for sacred use. (c) The verb rendered 'anoint' is nowhere else used of an activity that is either part of personal toilet or generous hospitality—there is another Hebrew word for that. *mšḥ* is strictly reserved for religious anointing, especially of the king (hence our derived word 'messiah') or, by extension, of priest and even prophet. The effective blasphemy of these revellers is placarded in the very Hebrew words that describe it. A modification of this approach has been proposed in recent years: both the religious terminology and the celebratory extravagance have been related to a single institutional base—the *marzeaḥ*. (This may have been a select brotherhood with particular concern for funerary rites.)

(6) Two footnotes complete our scamper through the texts. *Amos* 6.12a derides Israel's behaviour as the height of absurdity. Then it seem to me as if the last, almost 'throw-away' words of *8.6* charge the

powerful corn-merchants with a loathsome and quite gratuitous insult:

> 'Selling the weak for a silver coin
> and the poor for the sake of a pair of sandals
> —even the refuse of the grain shall we sell.'

Do they not liken their human merchandise to the very sweepings of the floor, which is all their victims can afford?

c. There has been little scholarly discussion of the originality and authenticity of Amos's social and ethical protests. But a different situation obtains in connection with his *religious critique*. In fact it is also a matter of hot debate just what the relevant texts are about, whether composed by Amos or not. These have been particularly worrying to many representatives of the successor religious traditions in Judaism and Christianity.

From our introductory standpoint it is useful to note just how the very openness of these few texts to remarkably different interpretations forces us to admit how little our studies to this point have contributed in terms of background information that we might call on to limit the available options.

(1) The first three relevant texts, though we meet them separately, form an apparent group—4.4-5; 5.4-6, 14-15. Each is largely composed of a series of commands; and each treats the theme of its predecessor from a new point of view.

Dispute over proper interpretation begins at the very beginning. 'Come to Bethel and rebel' (4.4): (i) Does this imply that rebels are not welcome at the sanctuary, or is it the very act of attending the sanctuary that constitutes the rebellion? (ii) Do Bethel and Gilgal stand for sanctuaries in general, or are these particular sacred spots problematic in and for themselves? (iii) How much weight is to be attached to the possessive in *your* sacrifices and tithes? Is God disowning interest in such religious practices altogether, and blaming the people for creating a religion out of their own whims (end of v. 5)?

'Seek me and live' (5.4b) is clearly opposed to seeking these just-mentioned sanctuaries. Beersheba has now been added to them, excluding the possibility that Amos the Judaean southerner rejected all northern Israelite shrines as inauthentic for worship of Yahweh, yet leaving the option open that Amos's hidden agenda 'between the lines' might involve partisanship for the temple in Jerusalem as the only true place of worship. Why is it that Beersheba is only more briefly mentioned, while Bethel and Gilgal are returned to and punned on? Is it just that the names Bethel and Gilgal were easier to play with? It was simple to suggest a mischievous connection between *glgl* and the Hebrew verb *glh*, 'to be exiled'. Then Bethel was either a near neighbour to or an alternative name for a place called (Beth-)On; and the Hebrew spelling of that name (*'wn*) could be 'misunderstood' for the noun *'awen* meaning 'trouble'.

It is often noted that v. 6 moves to talk about Yahweh in the third person, and sometimes claimed that this represents a second and editorial stage in the composition of the unit. It may be so; yet two observations deserve to be made in reply. The one is that the palistrophic structure already noted in our previous chapter includes v. 6. The other is that the balance between the opening 'seek me' and closing 'seek Yahweh' may be artistically deliberate: the opening 'me' could refer to Amos or Yahweh; the closing 'Yahweh' shows that he (ultimately at least) is intended, but leaves open the question at least of whether Amos is the appropriate medium for consultation of Yahweh.

Even without the following 5.14-15 we might have supposed that 'seek me and live' (5.4) was shorthand for 'seek me in order to live'. The final panel of this triptych leaves us in no doubt. Similarly, while the warnings against resort to Bethel and Gilgal might have been covert propaganda for Jerusalem, this is rendered much less likely when seeking me/Yahweh is further explained as seeking good and not evil, or even more passionately and precisely as hating evil and loving good: not just in pious but ineffective intention, but in the struggle for right and for rule of law in the public eye of the home community (5.15).

Such a reading of 5.14-15 seems to me to weaken gravely Coote's objection to the authenticity of these verses on the grounds that the choice they offer is expressed in words too general for the authentic Amos—and in too hopeful terms too. Comment is appropriate on this second objection of Coote's as well. Two aspects of v. 15b make me cautious over agreeing with him. First, 'perhaps' can be differently understood: either hopefully, or as warning against over-optimism. Then 'remnant' may have sounded more hopeful to the Jewish community after the exile (or to us when it refers to a fabric remainder that can still be marketed) than it did to Amos. Understood in the light of Amos 2.14-16, that picture of the catastrophe from which only the most heroic of the valiant could escape—and even he 'by the skin of his teeth', weaponless and stripped naked,—the left-over remnant is a much less optimistic image, whose bleakness is well echoed in Amos 3.12 and 5.18-20. Establishing or erecting justice at the gate is so concrete a counter-move to casting it on the ground (5.7) that there is a strong a priori case for authorship by Amos.

A rather different approach is ably advocated by Tromp, in the fine rhetorical analysis referred to in the last chapter. He could not be aware of Coote's work. But I feel that if he had known it he might have charged it with a naive approach to Amos's own intentions. Many of Amos's words are very bleak: their surface meaning can be read no other way. But is their intent simply at worst to jeer at those on their way to deserved perdition, or at best to annotate their record and arraign them before capital sentence is carried out? Or is the purpose of Amos's sharp criticism to shock his people into self-understanding *and a commitment to amelioration?* He refuses to commit his God to a positive response, but he does leave the door open.

(2) A whole bundle of questions cluster round Amos 5.21-24. Their elucidation belongs better in the commentaries than here. But it may be useful for us at least to list some of them. Many scholars treat vv. 21-24 as an originally separate and complete piece, to be compared with other prophetic 'purple passages' of cultic critique such as Isa. 1.10-17, Hos. 6.1-8, Mic. 6.6-8, and Jer. 7.21-23. However Koch, as we saw towards the end of the previous chapter, has recently sought to advance Lindblom's case that v. 21 simply continues what is begun in vv. 18-20: these have no concluding formula, and vv. 21ff. have no introductory one. The cultic practices criticized in 21-24 amount to a misuse of the 'day of the Lord' (vv. 18-20) which is itself a term for the great annual religious festival.

Then there has been lively discussion over the relation between vv. 21-24 and the three verses that conclude the chapter. The majority hold that vv. 25-27 represent subsequent additions to the basic core, but that v. 25 in particular does not misrepresent the drift of Amos's own thought. Some see this retrospect to the wilderness period as the first stage in the supplementation, followed by the addition of vv. 26-27; others consider v. 27 prior to vv. 25-26. However even that does not exhaust the agenda for debate. It is not agreed which English tense is appropriate for the verb in v. 26: if it is past ('and/but you carried') there is a close link to the retrospective reference of the preceding verse; but if it is future ('you will carry') then the threat of the exile to come has already begun, although it only becomes fully explicit in the last verse.

Whatever our answers to any of these questions, it seems to me that reading vv. 21-24 in the light of either vv. 18-20 or vv. 25-27 inevitably draws even more attention to the word 'your' in the central verses. The practices of those addressed are contrasted with an authentic or appropriate approach to the 'day of the Lord' and are aligned with worship of alien gods. Unless this is rhetorical exaggeration, we are directed to a reading of the central verses according to which Israel's religious practice is not simply deficient in ethical concern but is fundamentally corrupt.

(3) Before we leave this review of the texts, some further mention should be made of J. Lust's discussion of the redaction of Amos 5.4-6, 14-15. He gathers a number of linguistic comparisons which suggest a late monarchic or exilic date for these passages, especially the second of them. Prominent among these is the mention in vv. 4-6 of 'seeking' and 'coming', which are also the key verbs in Deut. 12.5, at the heart of the passage dealing with the centralization of worship which is widely held to refer to Jerusalem and to constitute a charter for the reform in the time of King Josiah. In similar vein is the choice between good and evil which he discerns in 5.14-15, and which he compares with Deuteronomistic choice, as in 'See I have set before you this day life and good, death and evil' (Deut. 30.15). Of course his case is a cumulative one, and will have to be weighed carefully by all serious readers of the texts. I can only admit to finding demand rather than choice in 5.14-15, and to wondering whether Deuteronomy 12 might not be influenced by Amos 5 rather than the other way round.

In fact I would suggest that, despite the similarity in language, the interests of Amos 5 and of Deuteronomy are very different: and perhaps deliberately so, even if Lust is correct that Amos 5.14-15 are later than Amos himself. It may be that Deuteronomy's call for allegiance to a central sanctuary was answered and rejected by those who preserved the Amos tradition, and who reaffirmed in 5.14-15 the authentic Amos's message (4.4-5 and 5.4-6) which placed right living above any commitment to temple.

2. **Problems**

We may restrict ourselves to three approaches in our attempt at historical assessment. The first of these is the contribution of the social sciences, especially anthropology and social history. The next is the evidence of archaeology. And the last is more linguistic: a renewed attention, partly in the light of these, to the proper meanings of the Hebrew terms for 'poverty' and 'justice'.

a. Sociological and anthropological analyses of the Hebrew Scriptures are no new enterprise. It is already some sixty-five years since the death of Max Weber, perhaps the greatest pathfinder in the field of sociology. However it is the case that such studies are very much 'in vogue' again amongst biblical scholars, and—within the English-speaking world at least—especially in North America.

It has to be admitted that there exists a good deal of mutual suspicion, and even occasional antipathy, between the majority of biblical scholars whose approach to the prophets remains the largely traditional blend of linguistic and textual studies in the service of the history of (religious) ideas, and the minority with some expertise in social history who direct many fresh and unfamiliar questions to their texts. The former group suspect the latter of coming too quickly and naively to highly complex texts; the latter often respond that many of the humanists' long-felt difficulties simply disappear in the light of sociological realism.

Part of the problem is that the whole range of *possibly* relevant data is too large and complex for the single scholar to encompass and control; and so short-cuts are taken which critics on one side or the other will properly censure. As we have noted before, one of the attractions of testing various approaches on the book of Amos is that it is short enough to permit a readier conspectus of the significant issues.

b. Archaeological background to our understanding of the prophets' critique of their society has been usefully reviewed recently by the Dutch scholar de Geus. He offers his own fresh perspective on the long-standing question of how far Israel's social structures were determined by purely internal factors such as her religion and how far by external ones (often simply described as 'Canaanite'). He notes first the almost complete lack of concern within Palestinian archaeology with a series of questions regularly faced in contemporary archaeology elsewhere about the general level of well-being and local variations within that level. Put simply: can terms such as 'rich' and 'poor' be clarified by excavation of material remains?

De Geus notes that excavations have disclosed that the ninth century BCE marked the high-point for royal building projects. There were no new ones after this century, although the prominent central buildings did continue in use till the collapse of Israel in the later eighth century and Judah in the early sixth. In the south there is some evidence of an increase in population towards the end of the period; but the dominant picture overall is of stagnation and impoverishment. And the pottery evidence parallels precisely that of the architecture.

His own reconstruction is as follows. The tenth century still evidences a mainly self-sufficient agrarian economy. However the new (royal) residences and other public buildings of the late tenth and ninth centuries had to be paid for. This did not in itself provoke an economic crisis since the first generations of royal taxes were largely spent within the country and because the centres were flourishing. However it was a new merchant and artisan class which profited from the changed structures, and many of these were originally non-Israelite. Economic decline did become acute later, as tax revenues were increasingly alienated into the hands of foreign empires.

This is a rather different picture from the general account so often repeated in studies of Amos: that he spoke against a background of recent if not contemporary new prosperity related to prolonged peace and security under King Jeroboam II. And if it is a fair reconstruction, then some of Amos's strictures may have to be assessed against a rather longer perspective than is often supposed.

c. A very persuasive account of the various terms for 'poverty' in the Hebrew Bible has been offered in a German study by a Brazilian pastor, M. Schwantes, on 'The Right of the Poor'. He notes that four main terms make up the Hebrew Bible's family of poverty, *raš*, *dal*, *'ani* and *'ebyon*. All except the first occur throughout the Bible; however *raš*, used in pithy descriptions of the feckless fellow who is often responsible for his own 'poverty', is in fact restricted to the Wisdom Literature. The other members of the group, quite variously translated even within any one of the standard translations of the scriptures, all have overtones of 'affliction', 'want', 'reduction' in status, and the like; and all three parts of the biblical canon emphasize their rights and the responsibility of others towards them. In the 'Book of the Covenant' they are 'Yahweh's people'; sacral regulations insist that all are alike in the practice of the cult; the prophets reinforce these views in many different ways; and the Wisdom literature too demonstrates that those who are *dal*, *'ani*, or *'ebyon* do have rights and that God makes himself responsible for their care.

'Religion' is one of the most difficult terms to use in critical discussion, for it means so many different things to different people. However two important results of the work of Schwantes for our purposes are these: poverty and riches made no official difference in the practice of 'religion' or cult; and the poor did not just possess notional rights in society but were actually held to have Yahweh as their champion.

On one important religious element of the biblical talk about poverty I have so far remained silent. It is noticeable that at least in later biblical texts, from the post-exilic period, some of the language of 'poverty' was more obviously 'religious' or 'spiritual' in sense. This is clearest in the case of *'ani* and the related *'anaw*, often to be rendered 'humble' rather than 'poor'. It is very likely that this shift in sense occurred in the wake of the destruction of the states of Israel and Judah with the resultant exile for many and despoliation for the remainder. All of the people were now in fact economically poor and socially deprived; and they welcomed the confirmation by their exilic prophets of the old doctrine that Yahweh espoused the cause of the poor. Since the 'Judaism' that survived this disaster was more of a religious community than an independent state even in Judah, let alone in exiled dispersion, it was natural that their dejection become understood in overt religious terms.

It was at least from this stage in Jewish tradition that the language of 'poverty' became formally ambiguous: it continued to refer to economic hardship; but it also decribed a chosen spiritual role that could *but need not* include material poverty. The issue is nicely illustrated in the similar but different Beatitudes in the Gospels of Luke and Matthew: 'blessed are the poor' and 'blessed are the poor in spirit'.

d. Our discussion up to this point in the volume has simply accepted the usual view that 'justice' and 'righteousness' as normally understood are appropriate translations for Hebrew *mišpaṭ* and *ṣedaqah*. However this has recently been questioned by Koch. He claims that research into these terms is in a state of flux; but he presents interim conclusions about which he is confident.

He insists that the terms refer to spheres of activity and to powers of Yahweh, and not simply to ethical or legal abstracts. It is no accident that they are often mentioned in connection with the cult. Sacrifice and sacred meals had been held to make these forces available to the worshippers, as in a sacrament. *mišpaṭ* and *ṣedaqah* are sometimes described as a fluid (Amos 5.24) that can be poured out healingly. These 'efficacious auras . . . not only surround the individual agent but also radiate out to the whole land, creating harmony between society and nature'. In surrounding Canaanite religion such forces were treated as gods. 'When Israel took over the language of Canaan, it rejected the ritual veneration of forces of this kind and gave them a new function as Yahweh's active powers. But since Israel went on using Canaanite words which carried this significance, it was unable to turn living deities into mere abstract concepts simply from one day to the next.'

It seems to me that more evidence will need to be produced before this case can win acceptance. It is not immediately obvious to me that 'justice' and 'righteousness' do generally appear in a cultic context, or that we should now assume such a context most times we meet these words. Yet talk within Christian theology of 'receiving grace' and 'being in grace' is not very distant from what Koch is attempting to depict.

Further Reading

The standard commentaries should be reviewed for their notes on the details of the various texts mentioned in this chapter.

Much of Coote's *Amos* is relevant to this topic, especially pp. 11-45, 73-86.

The fullest recent discussion of the view that the religious overtones of the protest in Amos 6.1-7 derive simply from the *marzeaḥ* organization which is mentioned in 6.7 is in

Barstad, *Religious Polemics*, 127-38.

The discussion in Koch's *Prophets* is in pp. 44-62, and is undergirded by the analysis in

K. Koch, 'Die Entstehung der sozialen Kritik bei den Propheten', H.W. Wolff (ed.), *Probleme Biblischer Theologie*, 1971, 236-57.

Sociological perspectives are much to the fore in the following:

Petersen, *Roles*.
R.R. Wilson, *Prophecy and Society in Ancient Israel*, Philadelphia: Fortress, 1980.
L. Epsztein, *Social Justice in the Ancient Near East and the People of the Bible*, London: SCM, 1986.

Wilson's work has drawn quite a lot of criticism; a useful sample is

B.O. Long, 'The Social World of Ancient Israel', *Interpretation* 36 (1982), 243-55.

Long himself is a very sensitive judge of the relevance of social studies to the literature of the Bible. His article on 'Prophetic Authority as Social Reality', G.W. Coats & B.O. Long (eds.), *Canon and Authority*, 1977, 3-20, was mentioned in Chapter 3 above.

Accurate social description is also helpfully attempted in

B. Lang, *Monotheism and the Prophetic Minority*, Sheffield: Almond, 1983—NB especially Chapter 4, which draws heavily on the book of Amos.

A large-scale sociological introduction to the Hebrew Bible by Norman Gottwald is promised shortly, and should help refocus attention on these topics. (His contentious *The Tribes of Yahweh: A Sociology of the Religion of Liberated Israel, 1250–1050 BCE*, London: SCM, 1980, is also reviewed well in Long, 'Social World'.)

Problems relating to the historical background are discussed in

J.H. Hayes & J.M. Miller (eds.), *Israelite & Judaean History*, London: SCM, 1977, 381-434,

while the lone archaeological discussion of the material background to prophetic social criticism is

J.K. de Geus, 'Die Gesellschaftskritik der Propheten und die Archäologie', *ZDPV* 98 (1982), 50-57.

Material issues are however also to the fore in

M.A. Cohen, 'The Prophets as Revolutionaries', *Biblical Archaeology Review* (1979), 12-19.
J. Sowada, 'Let Justice Surge Like Water . . .', *The Bible Today* 19 (1981), 301-305.

J.G. Bailey, 'Amos: Preacher of Social Reform', *idem*, 306-13.

For the German reader, the following are also of considerable interest and importance:

W. Dietrich, *Israel und Kanaan: vom Ringen zweier Gesellschafts-systeme*, Stuttgart: Verlag Katholisches Bibelwerk, 1979.

O. Keel, 'Rechttun oder Annahme des drohenden Gerichts?', *BZ* 21 (1977), 200-18.

M. Schwantes, *Das Recht der Armen* (BbET 4), 1977, 87-99.

R. Smend, 'Das Nein des Amos', *EvTh* 23 (1963), 404-23.

E. Würthwein, 'Kultpolemik oder Kultbescheid? Beobachtungen du dem Thema "Prophetie und Kult"', in E. Würthwein & O. Kaiser (eds.), *Tradition und Situation*, Göttingen, 1963, 115-31.

7

THE MESSAGE
OF AMOS

BEFORE WE stand back a little and comment on the wider religious and theological contribution of the book of Amos, we should first remind ourselves of relevant points already made. We have already had occasion in the previous chapter to note that 'religion' has many facets, and indeed means different things to different people. That simply reinforces the need to be quite specific in what we say about Amos's significance in this field.

a. We saw first that he had had dread visions of divine menace towards Israel, which culminated in disaster for an altar. That means at least that his view of reality included God; and also the realization that Yahweh, whom Israel served as *their* God, could envisage an end to *his* people's existence. Yet, as we noted, his 'God-talk' consists in hints rather than predictions, in images rather than definitions.

b. We deduced next that Amos did not regard himself as a 'prophet', that he did not claim status as a 'religious' functionary, that he did not require a position in popular or official religion to say what he had to say. (However, in the end, this biblical title was finally accorded to him.) He appears rather to have held that *anyone* who had heard Yahweh speak should himself 'prophesy': that means, speak out with the freedom prophets use. He appears to have been an agriculturalist. Yet our main evidence for him is as communicator: and he certainly was extraordinarily skilful in his use of words.

c. His opening sally on an Israel morally comfortable amid the international misbehaviour of her neighbours is a high point of the Bible's prophetic traditions. More eloquent than a theological essay, it makes two important religious moves: it claims Yahweh's sway over all the peoples of the Levant, and it guarantees a place within religious argument for common sense and basic decency.

d. At the end of our treatment of literary issues we left an important question unresolved: was Amos himself the author of the larger, more complex units of the book such as the first seventeen verses of chapter 5? Now, after our review of some of the individual elements of Amos's social and religious critique, we can return to this question and carry its discussion one stage further. We have detected no tension between the 'compositions' such as the opening chapters, or 4.6ff. and 5.1-17, or the visions, on the one side and their constituent parts on the other. In fact it is too grudging to say that we detect no tension: the wholes and parts complement and reinforce each other excellently. There may be no need to postulate in these sections the activity of a different 'hand'.

e. Then our last discussion suggested how intimately ethical and cultic concerns intersect in Amos's words. Some of the crimes featured in the opening complaints against Israel appear particularly heinous, because they concern Yahweh's holy name and altar. And it is all the more appropriate that the fifth vision should use destruction of the temple as symbol of the beginning of the end for the people. The sorts of evil that concern him need no subtle definition: distant crowds of foreigners could detect what was going on in Samaria—it was nothing less than violence taking over the throne. There must have already been an ethical component in the popular religion of his day; yet Amos raises this to a new importance with his insistence that to seek Yahweh is to hate evil, to love good, and to work publicly for what is right.

2. **Yahweh is His Name: The 'Doxologies'**

If only because this is our last chapter and last chance, it seems appropriate now to turn rather fuller attention to three important passages (4.13; 5.8-9; 9.5-6) which we have already discussed more briefly at beginning and end of Chapter 5. Each appears at a strategic point. The first and third follow two of the compositions in Amos whose 2 + 2 + 1 structure we have already noted: the one ends chapter four (v. 13) with its series of five disasters in vv. 6-11; the other, in 9.5-6, caps the fifth and last in the series of visions. We have already considered whether the second of them in 5.8-9 should be seen as the very focus of 5.1-17, or as an ironic anticipation and reinforcement of the coming threat in vv. 11-12 of that chapter. A number of questions cluster round these three passages. How do they relate to their immediate contexts? Do they go back to Amos himself? What are they modelled on?

a. It has long been argued that this series of so-called 'doxologies' are fragments of a longer hymn available to Amos, or more likely to a later editor of the book. Certainly they have similar content: they concern the god of the skies, or heavenly god, who makes the stars, who controls light and darkness, who brings rain and influences the rising and falling levels of the Nile. And the statements they make are expressed largely in the same manner: by Hebrew participles, which are a common feature of hymns of praise. That heavenly god, all three passages say, is called Yahweh. Was this thought novel to Amos, or to whichever later editor contributed the three pieces? Or was there a particular reason for strengthening the argument at these three points with a reminder of Yahweh's cosmic dimensions? Do they represent a climax or a post-script?

b. Each underscores just what sort of god Israel has to deal with, just what god Amos is warning Israel about. Seen this way, it seems to me, they resemble at least in function a strategic element in that other major composition that opens the book. After threatening first Israel's neighbours, and then Israel herself, Yahweh observes (2.9) that it was he who had destroyed the Amorites root and branch before Israel and given the latter their land. At a single stroke, all the foregoing threats become even more menacing: what Yahweh has already done to the Amorites, he can do again to any of Israel's neighbours; what Yahweh has already done for Israel in Canaan, he can now do against her in the same land. Here, as in the three hymn-like pieces, people are invited to take seriously the political implications of what they all too casually recite in cultic praise and confession.

The complementarity of the opening two chapters on the one side and these three compositions strengthened by the 'doxologies' on the other can be described another way as well. The book opens with the most eloquent of testimonies that Yahweh, worshipped by Israel, demands common morality of her neighbours too. The three compositions in question represent the other side of the same coin: that 'Yahweh' is none other than the name of the high god. This is no philosophically worked through definition of monotheism; but it is already pregnant with that future.

c. That is the continuing religious significance of these hymn-like pieces. Yet can we go further and locate this 'theological' implication historically? Can we attribute these verses to Amos, or must we set them in a later period? The argument has several distinct elements.

(1) A few points can be made from a literary angle. All three 'doxologies' do reinforce the message of their contexts: if later additions, they are good ones. On the other side, in the case of the first and third, they follow verses (4.12 and 9.4) which can themselves be readily interpreted as strong conclusions to the compositions of which they are a part. And, of course, Amos 5.8-9 is quite vital to the elaborate structure of that chapter. If Amos 5.1-17 is judged too complex or too literary to be a product of the historical Amos, then the possibility is greater that Amos 4.13 and 9.5-6 are also sensitive contributions by one of his successors.

(2) Also relevant are the dates, if we can ascertain them, of similar materials in the Old Testament. Quite the closest similarities in hymn-like content are to be found in Job 9.5-10. These verses are a small part of a much longer speech in which Job portrays the unknowableness of God:

> Lo, he passes by me, and I see him not;
> > he moves on, but I do not perceive him (v. 11).
>
> If it is not he, who then is it? (v. 24b).

We can only speculate about the reasons for the links between Job 9 and the Amos 'doxologies'. If each is simply adopting and adapting a hymnic tradition common to both, then we have no leverage on the dating issue. If the Amos verses are naming Job's mysterious God as 'Yahweh', then they will be later than at least that part of the book of Job. Yet that relative date is hard to make more precise. Job has often been considered an exilic or post-exilic book: partly because it is in the third and least structured part of the canon of the Hebrew Bible, and partly because its crises and arguments are held to reflect Judaean self-examination after the national catastrophe at the beginning of the sixth century BCE. Yet both assumptions are open to serious question; and a monarchic date for the book can be readily defended—whether earlier than Amos in mid-eighth century is another matter.

'The Lord (of Hosts) is his name' is a surprisingly rare phrase in the Bible. In fact, outside Amos, it occurs only within Isaiah 40–55 (the so-called Second Isaiah) and in Jeremiah. Of the four Isaiah passages (47.4; 48.2; 51.15; 54.5) the third is most similar to the Amos 'doxologies':

> For I am the Lord your God,
>> who stirs up the sea so that its waves roar—
>> the Lord of hosts is his name.

Then, of the eight Jeremiah passages, it is Jer. 31.35-36 which represents the most striking parallel:

> Thus says the Lord,
> who gives the sun for light by day
>> and the fixed order of the moon and stars for light by night,
> who stirs up the sea so that its waves roar—
> the Lord of hosts is his name:
> If this fixed order departs from before me, says the Lord,
> then shall the descendants of Israel cease
> from being a nation before me for ever.

Several of the other Jeremiah examples come from the later chapters which are regularly ascribed to Jeremiah's successors rather than himself: in them 'the Lord is his name' seems little more than a conventional thing to say.

d. One or two suggestions can be made on the basis of these connections: One is that 'the Lord is his name' does not derive from the book of Job or from the praise of God in the Psalms, but has been developed in a prophetic milieu. Then it is common to all three contexts, Amos, Jeremiah, and (Deutero-)Isaiah, that Yahweh's heavenly and creative power is recalled to remind us of his ability both to destroy and to rescue his people. And finally, and unhappily, we are no further forward in our discussion of whether these verses are original to Amos himself. His words could be the source on which his two successors draw. Equally these verses could have been added to the book of Amos between one and two centuries later, in a period when we know their sentiments were current. I cannot avoid the conclusion that the key to the whole issue is locked in the unusual structure of Amos 5.1-17.

3. **Poetry: Precision and Openness**

Some will be surprised that I draw attention to the poetry of the book
of Amos in a discussion of its religious and theological significance.
They may sympathize with a senior member of Edinburgh University
who asked the Dean of the Faculty of Divinity after he had offered a
piece from T.S. Eliot as the prayer to open the Senatus Academicus,
'Dean, was that a prayer or a poem?'

The issue I am trying to identify is whether the poetic quality of
Amos is simply the medium in which he communicates, or whether it
is also part of what he seeks to communicate. It cannot be gainsaid
that most of the biblical prophets uttered balanced rhythmical pieces
which are structured like Israel's classics of hymn and learning in the
Psalms and Wisdom books. Yet what may we fairly deduce from this?

a. In some sense, these 'prophets' shared or adopted the traditions
and language and forms of praise and discussion that were current
among their contemporaries. How much choice did they have? Was
this alignment a deliberate strategy? Were they closer to the 'cult'
and the 'schools' than to other sectors in society? Or was it perhaps
precisely these groups and their claims and influence they wanted to
confront? Were formal, balanced, terse lines simply the proper mode
for public address in that society? We have insufficient information
about the period to answer these questions with any certainty. Yet to
ask enough of them should prevent us from rushing to unwarranted
assumptions.

b. Even more important than the formal aspect of 'prophetic' poetry
is the quality of its language. There is little talk in Amos and his
contemporaries of 'the word' or 'the word of the Lord'. Yet they do
come across to us as craftsmen with words. Our regular view is of the
prophet as divine messenger or ambassador; and indeed this is the
developed biblical view too. Yet when we use this language we must
be careful to think back to a day when diplomacy was conducted
much less by detailed messages passing between heads of government
electronically via satellite, whether actually presented by an ambassador
or not, but by ambassadors and ministers plenipotentiary who
enjoyed considerable discretion in the development of policy and its
formulation. If that historical succession of poetic critics from Amos
to Jeremiah was later re-presented as a succession of 'servants' and
'emissaries' duly acknowledged by God, then this implies the

recognition that they had in fact been good advocates of his cause.

Amos and his ilk sought to convince by argument, rather than compel by authority. Amos makes his appeal to Israel not in terms of divine revelation old or new, but by an invidious point-to-point comparison of her behaviour with that of her neighbours who (she knew) broke all natural norms. So telling is his language as he surveys Israel's social and religious shortcomings that his accusations once made are unanswerable. As with all good poetry, his use of the Hebrew language purifies it: whether by returning words back to their proper sense away from conventional misuse, or by a novel clash of ideas where the best of the old was not enough. One of the striking qualities of words in the hands of a poet is that they are more exact and precise than the careful definitions of an expert draughtsman or scientist.

c. Yet another poetic quality tends in the opposite direction, without in any sense negating what has just been said. An important aspect of poetry, indeed perhaps the defining characteristic of great poetry is its universality, its appeal to many succeeding generations and to circles quite foreign to its own first production. Part of the importance for us of these biblical critics is the quality of their words. The deftness of their statements has achieved classical status. Their ability to comprehend moments in their own situation and catch them in the right words is easily conceded to be a god-given gift.

I think this might be my part-answer to Stephen Geller's interesting question about the propriety of calling the prophets 'poets'. He is quite clear that they deserve the title on the grounds of their use of language; but appears embarassed that such a title might compromise their status as mediators of the divine word. His own attempt at a resolution of the religious problem is based on the doctrine of creation: if everything was created by the divine word, then 'all words are divine creations'.

4. Religion as Cult

It is at this point that we have to be most careful in our use of the word 'religion'. If we use the term widely enough, say in the popular sense of anything that has to do with God, then Amos is a religious figure; and part of his message is that 'religion' is not to be confused with 'cult', that 'being religious' involves more than observing certain specifically religious (= cultic) practices. If we use 'religion' in the narrower sense, restricting it to what we have just called the 'specifically religious', then Amos was either anti-religious or critically religious.

We noted in our second chapter that his final vision, of destruction beginning at the altar, could be relevant for establishing his religious attitudes. Unfortunately the scene may be ambiguous. Is the temple chosen for the beginning of the attack because it is the very symbol of the people's false self-confidence? Or does Yahweh first destroy his normal channel of communication with his people, rather like a belligerent government recalling its diplomatic representatives at the outbreak of war? Two further points seem worth making.

a. One is that there are and often have been strands both in Judaism and in Christianity which have been more or less a-cultic. And these have taken comfort and inspiration from Amos and kindred elements in the prophetic tradition. One thinks of many Israelis and other Jews too who see no essential role for religion in their lives. And one remembers the vital witness of the Society of Friends.

b. Yet if I were pressed to supply a not-too-illicit 20th-century analogy for Amos's attitude to religion, I would recommend pondering part of the elusive but haunting legacy of the imprisoned Dietrich Bonhoeffer, with his talk of 'religionless Christianity'. In many ways he was a conservative theologian. He was a churchman who prayed, and who to the end made the liturgy available to his fellow prisoners. Yet religious *ordinance* was not the *essence* of his Christianity. And he was in revolt against a national church which preferred to sanction governmental expediency rather than expose and combat injustice. It may well be that Amos's attitudes to 'religion' were similarly nuanced.

5. Hope at the End

There is a tension built into the text of Amos which seems impossible to resolve however it is looked at. At the conclusion of a message which has been consistently cautionary—at its best 'straight from the shoulder' and at its worst downright bleak—come five verses that kindle hope. They talk of a revived Davidic dominion, luxuriant agriculture, and an inviolable resettlement of Israel on its land. At

their surface meaning the words in Amos 9.11-15 run counter to
Amos's expressions elsewhere: most strikingly, v. 14b contradicts
5.11b. Any special position of Israel amongst the nations seems to
have been excluded as recently as in 9.7. Then, even if we hold that
his repeated dire warnings were intended to jolt those who heard
them into a change for the better and return to Yahweh, must we not
conclude that these final verses endanger the whole strategy?

Such a move from negative to positive and introduced by 'in that
day' (9.11) and 'behold, the days are coming' (9.13) is part of a much
wider pattern in classical biblical prophecy. In a book such as Isaiah,
whose very name (*yeša'-yahu*) can be interpreted as meaning 'Yahweh
is deliverance', the discussion of the authenticity of such positive
materials is much more intractable. This is partly because hopeful
and bleak sentiments are in better balance there, and partly because
some of the dreams in Isaiah have a specially hallowed place in
Christian theology. An attempt was made to camouflage this new
theme in Amos by adding the words 'except that I will not utterly
destroy the house of Jacob' to the original 9.8 and claiming authority
for the added words with the tailpiece 'says the LORD' (cf. the end of
vv. 12 and 15). Yet its jerky introduction cannot be disguised.
Equally this again makes any conclusions won from study of Amos a
useful yardstick in other research.

6. Postscript

The point just made happens to return us to where we began: Amos's
vital place not just for ongoing 'religious' thought and practice, but
also for the critical appraisal of other parts of the biblical past as well.
We have taken one particular route through the book of Amos. Yet
others would have been quite as possible, for we have seen how
closely interconnected are its different themes. Decisions made and
options closed in considering any single one of them inevitably affect
our scrutiny of the others. And so it is with Amos as a whole within
the Prophets and indeed within the Bible as a whole.

Further Reading

A full treatment of the 'doxologies' in Amos can be found in three related
articles by J.L. Crenshaw:

'The Influence of the Wise upon Amos', *ZAW* 79 (1967), 42-51.

'Amos and the Theophanic Tradition', *ZAW* 80 (1968), 203-15.
'*YHWH Ṣeba'ot Šemo*: A Form-Critical Analysis', *ZAW* 81 (1969), 156-75.

A more recent review is available in

C.I.K. Story, 'Amos—Prophet of Praise', *VT* 30 (1980), 67-80.

That Job is prior to Deutero-Isaiah is argued in:

S. Terrien, 'Quelques remarques sur les affinités de Job avec le Deutero-Esaïe', *Volume du Congrès, Genève 1965* (SVT 15), 1966, 295-310.

The affinities of prophecy and wisdom are usefully discussed, with full bibliographies, in:

R.E. Clements, *Prophecy and Tradition*, Oxford: Blackwell, 1975, 73-86.
J.A. Emerton, 'Wisdom', G.W. Anderson (ed.), *Tradition and Interpretation*, Oxford: Clarendon, 1979, 214-37.
R.N. Whybray, 'Prophecy and Wisdom', R. Coggins, A. Phillips & M. Knibb (eds.) *Israel's Prophetic Tradition*, 1982, 181-99.

More specific links between Amos and Wisdom are discussed in:

S. Terrien, 'Amos and Wisdom', B.W. Anderson & W. Harrelson (eds.), *Israel's Prophetic Heritage*, London: SCM, 1962, 108-15.
Wolff, *Amos the Prophet*.

The relationship of prophecy and cult has been handled in:

R. Murray, 'Prophecy and the Cult', R. Coggins, A. Phillips & M. Knibb (eds.) *Israel's Prophetic Tradition*, 1982, 200-216.

Reference was made above to:

D. Bonhoeffer, *Letters and Papers from Prison*, London: Fontana, 1959 (e.g. pp. 122-25).
S.A. Geller, 'Were the Prophets Poets?', *Proof Texts* 3 (1983), 211-21.

Poetic language is usefully introduced in:

W. Nowottny, *The Language Poets Use*, London: Athlone Press, 1962.

The greater precision of poetic language is powerfully argued in:

G.D. Martin, *The Architecture of Experience*, Edinburgh: The University Press, 1981.

The integration of the closing verses of Amos is discussed in:

> Coote, 110-34.
> Koch, 1982, 69-76.
> Mays, 156-68.
> Wolff, 1977, 344-55.

- and further in:

> J. Bright, *Covenant and Promise*, London: SCM, 1977 (especially
> pp. 86-87).

Von Rad, 138, detects in them a theology current in Judah in the eighth century BCE. And Rudolph's major commentary closes with him acquiescing in the genuineness of Amos 9.11-15.

The preceding verses are usefully reviewed in

> H. Gese, 'Das Problem von Amos 9,7', *Textgemäss: FS E. Würthwein*,
> Göttingen: Vandenhoeck & Ruprecht, 1979, 33-38.

A popular attempt to correlate this post-exilic mitigation with our contemporary religious experience and longings can be read in:

> C.H. Miller, 'Amos and Faith Structures: A New Approach', *The
> Bible Today*, 19 (1981), 314-19.

A final and 'canonical' perspective on the matter is available in

> B.S. Childs, *Introduction to the Old Testament as Scripture*,
> London: SCM, 1979, 395-410.

INDEXES

INDEX OF BIBLICAL REFERENCES

INDEX OF SUBJECTS

INDEX OF AUTHORS